SECOND EDITION

The
iPhone
Book

How to do the most important,
useful & fun stuff with your iPhone

D0000087

Scott Kelby & Terry White

The iPhone Book, Second Edition

The iPhone Book Team

CREATIVE DIRECTOR
Felix Nelson

TRAFFIC DIRECTOR
Kim Gabriel

PRODUCTION MANAGER
Dave Damstra

TECHNICAL EDITORS
Kim Doty
Cindy Snyder

DESIGNER
Jessica Maldonado

STUDIO SHOTS
Scott Kelby
Terry White

STOCK PHOTOGRAPHY
COURTESY OF
iStockphoto.com

PUBLISHED BY
Peachpit Press

Composed in Myriad Pro, Lucida Grande, and Helvetica by Kelby Media Group.

Trademarks
All terms mentioned in this book that are known to be trademarks or service marks have been appropriately capitalized. Peachpit Press cannot attest to the accuracy of this information. Use of a term in the book should not be regarded as affecting the validity of any trademark or service mark.

iPhone, iPod, iTunes, Macintosh, and Mac are registered trademarks of Apple. Windows is a registered trademark of Microsoft Corporation.

Warning and Disclaimer
This book is designed to provide information about the iPhone. Every effort has been made to make this book as complete and as accurate as possible, but no warranty of fitness is implied.

The information is provided on an as-is basis. The authors and Peachpit Press shall have neither liability nor responsibility to any person or entity with respect to any loss or damages arising from the information contained in this book or from the use of the discs or programs that may accompany it.

ISBN 13: 978-0-321-57783-2
ISBN 10: 0-321-57783-3

9 8 7 6 5 4 3 2 1

Printed and bound in the United States of America

www.kelbytraining.com
www.peachpit.com

PRODUCED BY

Kelbymedia
GROUP INC

For Katherine and Elizabeth Moser:
two wonderful little gifts from above.
–SCOTT KELBY

For my mom, who always taught me to do the right thing,
and to my dad, who inspired me and pushed me to succeed.
–TERRY WHITE

Scott's Acknowledgments

This is the third book I've been lucky enough to co-author with Terry, and I can tell you from experience that the only downside of co-authoring a book with him is that I only get half as much space to thank all the wonderful people whose help, hard work, and support go into making a book like this.

To Kalebra: My wonderful, amazing, hilarious, fun-filled, super-gorgeous, and loving wife. Your spirit, warmth, beauty, brains, patience, and unconditional love continue to prove what everybody always says—I'm the luckiest guy in the world.

To Jordan & Kira: You two little bundles bring immeasurable joy to my life, and I'm so proud and tickled to be your dad. I couldn't ask for anything more.

To Jeff: You are the world standard that all brothers should be judged by. No wonder everybody loves you the way they do!

To my co-author Terry White: You're the one who convinced me to do this book, and without your many ideas, your influence, and your great writing, this book would never have seen the light of day. I'm truly honored to have shared these pages with you, and to count you among my very best friends.

To Kathy Siler (my secret weapon): Without you, I'd be sitting in my office mumbling and staring at the ceiling. Thanks for doing all the "hard work," and making my work life have calm, order, and sense, and for making it all a lot of fun. You are the best.

To my editor Kim Doty: I just love working with you. How can you not love working with someone who always has such a warm smile, such a great attitude, and does such great work? Thanks doesn't cover it…but…thanks.

To Cindy Snyder, Jessica Maldonado, and Dave Damstra (my book editing, design, and layout team): I just love working with you guys, and I'm constantly impressed and amazed at the quality of what you do, and how quickly you can do it.

To Felix Nelson, my brilliant Creative Director: What can I say—you are the best in the business, and ideas and art flow out of you like a Pez dispenser. I'm a very lucky guy to even get to work with you. Thank you, my friend, for everything you do for me, and our company.

To Dave Moser: Getting to work with my best buddy every day is definitely a blessing, but the way you're always looking out for me takes it to a whole new level. :-)

To Jean A. Kendra: Thanks for watching "the other side" of our business, and for being such a great friend over the years.

To Nancy Aldrich-Ruenzel, Ted Waitt, Scott Cowlin, and all my friends at Peachpit Press: Thank you for making the book-writing process virtually painless, and for having me as one of your authors.

To John Graden, Jack Lee, Dave Gales, Judy Farmer, and Douglas Poole: Your wisdom and whip-cracking have helped me immeasurably throughout my life, and I'm both grateful and totally in your debt.

To God and His son Jesus Christ: Thank you for always hearing my prayers, for always being there when I need You, for blessing me with such a wonderful joy-filled life, and such a warm, loving family to share it with.

Terry's Acknowledgments

It's not every day that I get to work on a project that is both challenging and fun at the same time. Writing a book such as this takes a lot of focus and attention to detail. Although there were many late nights and much time spent away from my family, they didn't complain once. I have an amazing wife who knows that one of my passions is technology and gadgets, so she completely understood when I said, "Hey, guess what? I'm going to co-author *The iPhone Book* with Scott!" Carla is my balance and she helps me in so many ways every day. I also have two amazing daughters: Ayoola is both smart and constantly focused on taking it to the next level. I see so much of myself in her at times that it's scary. My youngest daughter, Sala, has many of my other traits. She makes me laugh out loud every day and lives to enjoy life. They make those late nights, long weekends, and hectic travel schedules worthwhile, because at the end of the day, it's all for them anyway. I also have a great sister, Pam, who is the person I go to when I need advice. It's great having an older sibling and she's the best sister a guy could have.

I also have to thank all my "gadget buddies"! It's the guys and gals that I hang out with that inspire me to play and learn about gadgets of all kinds. My colleague Dave Helmly—we call him "Radar"—is probably more of a gadget freak than I am. Nine out of 10 times, when I call him to tell him about a new toy, he's already got one in his hands and starts telling me about it. My buddy Larry Becker is always calling me and letting me in on the latest gadget that he just heard about or got to play with. Special thanks to Jack Beckman and Chita Hunter for some last minute hot tips. Also, I thank my friends at my local Apple Store: Linda, Mike, Carol, Amir, Shaun, and Dave for constantly making me feel like a VIP when I walk in. And, of course, I have to thank all my friends who support me at my Macintosh users' group, MacGroup-Detroit, especially Mary, Joe, Calvin, Jack, Chita, Phyllis, Yvonne, Bill, Shirley & Shirley, Brian & Char, Loretta, Mia, Michele, Leonard, Mike, Aquil, and Harold.

Although I enjoy writing, it's not my full-time gig. I have the best job on the planet and work for the best company in the world. I have to give special thanks to my boss, Sue Scheen, who not only inspires me with her natural leadership abilities, but also gives me the freedom and the time off that I need to pursue my other technology and industry passions. I work with some of the smartest people in the industry, and I want to thank everyone at Adobe Systems, Inc., not only for providing the best software tools in existence but also for keeping me technically educated and motivated to achieve greatness.

Of course, I have to thank the guy who is probably my biggest source of inspiration, and that is one of my best friends and the co-author of this book, Scott Kelby. I'm constantly amazed at how much this guy accomplishes each year. There is no stopping him. Not only is he great in his career, but he's also a great father to his two beautiful kids and a great husband to his wonderful wife, Kalebra. I probably wouldn't have gotten into all this writing if it wasn't for Scott. Scott, you're an inspiration to us all! Thanks, buddy!

About the Authors

Scott Kelby

Scott is Editor-in-Chief and Publisher of *Photoshop User* magazine, and Editor-in-Chief and Publisher of *Layers* magazine. He is President and co-founder of the National Association of Photoshop Professionals (NAPP), the trade association for Adobe® Photoshop® users, and President of the software, education, and publishing firm Kelby Media Group.

Scott is a photographer, designer, and award-winning author of more than 50 books on technology and digital imaging, including the best-selling books: *The iPod Book*, *The Digital Photography Book (volumes 1 & 2)*, and *The Photoshop Book for Digital Photographers*. Scott has authored several best-selling Macintosh books, including the award-winning *Macintosh: The Naked Truth*, from New Riders, and *The Mac OS X Leopard Book* and *Mac OS X Conversion Kit* from Peachpit Press. His books have been translated into dozens of different languages, including Russian, Chinese, French, German, Spanish, Korean, Greek, Turkish, Japanese, Dutch, and Taiwanese, among others.

For the past four years straight, Scott has been awarded the distinction of being the world's No. 1 best-selling author of all computer and technology books, across all categories. His book, *The Digital Photography Book, volume 1* is the best-selling book on digital photography in history.

Scott is Training Director for the Adobe Photoshop Seminar Tour, Conference Technical Chair for the Photoshop World Conference & Expo, and is a speaker at trade shows and events around the world. For more information on Scott, visit his daily blog at www.scottkelby.com.

Terry White

Terry is the author of *Secrets of Adobe Bridge* from Adobe Press and co-author of *InDesign CS/CS2 Killer Tips*, from New Riders.

Terry is Director of North America Creative Pro Technical Sales for Adobe Systems, Inc., and has been with Adobe for over a decade, where he leads a team of solution engineers and product specialists that focus on professional publishing, Web authoring, and digital video/audio. Terry is both an Adobe Certified Expert and Creative Suite Master.

He has been active in the industry for over 20 years and is the founder and President of MacGroup-Detroit, Michigan's largest Macintosh users' group, and is a columnist for *Layers* magazine and *X-Ology Magazine*.

Terry is the host of the top-ranked *Adobe Creative Suite Video Podcast* and author of the world renown *Terry White's Tech Blog* (http://terry white.com/techblog), and is a key presenter at major industry shows around the world.

Table of Contents

Chapter Three 65

Please Mr. Postman
Getting (and Sending) Email on Your iPhone

Chapter Six   **141**

The Song Remains the Same
Using iTunes, the iTunes Store, and the App Store

Chapter Nine **211**

Cereal Killer
Killer Tips and Tricks

Chapter Ten 263

The Trouble with Boys
Troubleshooting Your iPhone

Seven Things You'll Wish You Had Known...

(1) The first chapter is for absolute beginners, so if you've had your iPhone for a few months and you already know how to turn it on, how to zoom in, how to navigate around, put it to sleep, etc., you can skip right over to Chapter 2 and start there. It won't hurt our feelings one bit (but you might want to at least skim through Chapter 1 anyway. Hey, ya never know).

(2) You don't have to read it chapter by chapter. Outside of that first I-just-opened-the-box chapter, we designed this book to be a "jump-in-anywhere" book. You don't have to read it in order, chapter by chapter, so if you want to learn how to do a certain thing, just find the topic in the Table of Contents, turn to that page, and you'll have the answer you need in seconds. Each page shows you how to do just one important thing. One topic. One idea. For example, if you want to learn how to delete an email, we will show you, step by step, how to do exactly that. No big discussions about email account protocols, or about server-side instructions—just how to delete an email message. That's it.

(3) We didn't totally "geek out." Terry and I wrote everything just as if a friend came over to our house, pulled out their new iPhone, and started asking us questions. So, for example, if you were at my house and you turned to me and said, "Hey Scott, is there a way to see more of this webpage on my screen?" I wouldn't go into how the iPhone's built-in vibrotactile actuator works. In real life, I'd turn to you and say, "Just turn your iPhone sideways and it switches to give you a wider view." I'd tell you short, sweet, and right to the point, just like that. So that's what we do throughout the book. It's not a "tell-me-all-about-it" book, instead it's a "show-me-how-to-do-it" book.

Before Reading This Book!

(4) There's a bonus video just for you. Terry and I shot a special video, and in it we give you some extra iPhone tips, show you some of our favorite accessories, and share some of the ways we use our iPhones, so once you're done reading the book, take a minute and check it out at **www.kelbytraining .com/books/iphone2**. You'll need a password to access the video. The password is **ringtone** (by the way, those that skip over this quick intro will never even know it's there. Plus, they'll all start with Chapter 1, even if this is their second iPhone, so it serves 'em right, eh?).

(5) The intro page at the beginning of each chapter is designed to give you a quick mental break, and honestly, they have little to do with the chapter. In fact, they have little to do with anything, but writing these off-the-wall chapter intros is kind of a tradition of mine (I do this in all my books), but if you're one of those really "serious" types, you can skip them because they'll just get on your nerves.

(6) There's also a bonus tips chapter in the book. Although we put lots of cool tips throughout the book, you can never have enough tips (stuff like little-known shortcuts, suggestions, or tricks that can make using your iPhone easier or more fun), so in this second edition of the book, there's now a special bonus chapter of nothing but "killer" tips (Chapter 9).

(7) If you have an iPod touch, you may realize that it's pretty much an iPhone without the phone, but everything else is nearly identical (they use the same iPod, calendar, contacts, email, Web browser, and even the iTunes App Store), so if you have an iPod touch, just skip the phone chapter (Chapter 2) and the stuff about the built-in camera.

Chapter One

The Bare Essentials

That Stuff You Have to Learn First

I was originally going to name this chapter *Basic Training* after the 1985 movie by the same name (or the 1971 version of *Basic Training*, or the 2006 version, which went straight to video despite the fact it starred The Rock). But I started to wonder how many people would actually read a chapter that has the word "basic" in the title. It's sad, but nobody really wants to learn the basics anymore—they want to jump into the deep end of the pool and start with some advanced techniques, because they figure the basic stuff is too basic for them. So basically, I thought instead about using the title from the movie *Basic Instinct*. Now, I never actually saw the movie myself (didn't it have Scatman Crothers in it?), but I heard it was better than *Basic Instinct 2*, which I think starred Carrot Top and Ernest Borgnine (but since I didn't see that one either, I can't swear they were actually in it). So I started thinking of a term that meant basics but didn't have the downside of the word basics, and I came up with "essentials." Because this chapter covers the essential stuff you'll need to really make the most of your iPhone, but "essentials" has no marketing flair. No pizzaz. No bling. (No bling?) So I thought, what device do American marketers use to capture the attention of today's most coveted demographic (people with credit left on their Visa cards), and then *Bare Essentials* (from the short-lived 1991 TV series of the same name) came to mind. It sounds just naughty enough to trick someone into reading it, but not so naughty that Snoop Dogg would read it. That brings up an interesting question. What are you doing here?

1

Turning Your iPhone On

To turn on your iPhone, press the Sleep/Wake button at the top of the iPhone (shown circled here in red). After a moment, the Apple logo will appear, and shortly after that you'll be greeted with the Home screen, which is pretty much your main jumping off point to all the different things the iPhone can do.

Putting Your iPhone to Sleep

If you want to put your iPhone to sleep (which is a great way to conserve battery life when you're not actively using any of the iPhone's functions), you just press the Sleep/Wake button on the top once (even though your iPhone is asleep, it will still receive calls and text messages as if it were on). When you put your iPhone to sleep, you'll hear a little click sound and your screen will go blank. While your iPhone is in this Sleep mode, the buttons on the screen are deactivated, so if you put the iPhone in your pocket (or purse), it won't accidentally come on and start playing a song, or a video, or doing anything that would waste battery time. To wake your iPhone from Sleep mode, you can either tap that button again, or press the Home button on the bottom center of your iPhone (just below the screen). When your iPhone wakes, the screen is still locked (just in case you awakened it accidentally). To unlock the screen, just press your finger lightly on the gray button with the right-facing arrow on the bottom left of the screen, slide it to the right, and the Home screen appears.

Turning Your iPhone Completely Off

If you want to turn your iPhone completely off (you won't receive phone calls or text messages), just press-and-hold the Sleep/Wake button on the top of the iPhone for a few seconds until the red Slide to Power Off button appears. To shut down, just take your finger, press lightly on that red button, and slide it to the right. Your screen will turn black, you'll see a small round status icon for just a moment, then your iPhone will power off.

Getting Stuff into Your iPhone with iTunes

The way you get music, videos, movies, ringtones, other applications, your address book, calendars, photos, etc., into your iPhone is through Apple's free software called iTunes (you must have version 7.7 or higher to work with your iPhone 3G) for Windows and Macintosh computers. Think of iTunes as the gateway between your computer and your iPhone.

Mac: If you have a Macintosh, iTunes comes preinstalled on every Mac (and has for years), so you've already got it (just make sure you have the latest version of iTunes by launching iTunes, and then going under the iTunes menu and choosing Check for Updates). When you plug your iPhone into your Mac (this is called "syncing"), it automatically launches iTunes and uploads any music, videos, photos, etc., you have in iTunes right into your iPhone (if you have this preference set).

Windows: If you're a Windows user, then you'll need to go to Apple.com/itunes and download the latest version of iTunes now (remember—iTunes is free software). Once you've downloaded and installed iTunes, you'll use it to manage and sort all your music, videos, movies, etc. (including anything you buy from the iTunes Store), and you'll use it to choose which songs, videos, movies, etc., actually get uploaded into your iPhone (there's a whole chapter on just how to do this. It's Chapter 6).

Getting Back to the Home Screen

There's only one "hard" button (an actual real button you can feel) on the face of the iPhone (it's found just below the touchscreen), and it's very important because with it you're only one click away from being back at the Home screen. Just press it, and the familiar Home screen appears (okay, it might not be that familiar right now, but don't worry—it will be sooner than you'd think). From then on, you'll use the touchscreen controls for navigating around your iPhone, making calls, playing music, and pretty much everything else the iPhone does.

Charging Your iPhone

Apple gives you two ways to charge your iPhone: (1) the AC power adapter (one end plugs into the dock connector at the bottom of your iPhone via the provided USB cable, and the other end plugs into a standard household outlet), or (2) your iPhone will charge any time it's connected to your computer with the USB cable (one end plugs into the dock connector, and the other end plugs into the USB port on your computer). (*Note:* There are other third-party charging solutions, like car chargers, but you have to buy those separately.) There is also a charging dock available from the Apple Store, which is nice because it stands your iPhone upright while it's charging (so you don't have to just lay your iPhone on a table) and offers an audio out plug to connect your iPhone to speakers or a stereo receiver, but other than that, there's no advantage to using the Dock over just plugging your iPhone directly into your computer (whether you use the Dock, the AC power adapter, or the USB cable by itself, they all work the same way. The only difference is, if you use the Dock, you plug the USB cable into the dock connector on the Dock, rather than the iPhone itself).

Adjusting the Volume

There are volume controls on the top-left side of your iPhone (shown circled here in red). By default, they control the ringer volume—each time you press the top button it increases the ringer volume, and the bottom button decreases the ringer volume with each press. When you change the ringer volume using these buttons, you'll see a volume bar temporarily appear onscreen so you can easily see your current volume setting as you adjust it. Although by default these buttons control the ringer volume, these are "context sensitive controls," so once you make a call, they automatically switch to control the volume of your phone call (that way, if you're making your call in a busy place like an airport, you can turn up the volume so you can hear your call). If you're playing a song or a video using the iPod functions, the buttons switch to control their volume.

iTip

If you're playing music on your iPhone, and find yourself turning the volume down fairly often, it probably just means you're too old. Sorry, that was lame. (I'd like to tell you that these little comments get funnier as the book goes on, but sadly they don't.)

Using Your iPhone's Built-In Speaker

If your Apple headphones (headset) are plugged in (they're actually called "earbuds"), then you'll hear your music, videos, and even phone calls directly through them. However, your iPhone also has its own speaker and anytime your earbuds aren't plugged in, that speaker is active (it has to be—otherwise you wouldn't hear your phone ring, right?). If you want to use your iPhone's speakerphone (when you're on a phone call), just tap the Speaker button that appears onscreen while your call is in progress. When you tap that button, it will turn solid blue to let you know the speakerphone is active. To turn the speakerphone off, tap that solid blue button again.

Your iPhone's Auto-Sleep Mode

Your iPhone is very careful to conserve battery power (actually, it's pretty much obsessed with it), so if you're not actively doing something with your iPhone, in about 45 seconds it dims the brightness of the screen (to save battery power), and then about 15 seconds later, if you still haven't done anything, it thinks you're busy doing something else and it puts itself to sleep (again, to save battery power). Waking your iPhone is easy (as noted earlier): just press the Home button or tap the Sleep/Wake button at the top of your iPhone.

Mini Icon Decoder

Your iPhone displays lots of little status icons across the very top of your iPhone's touch-screen to help you know what's going on in its world. For example, the little bars on the top left show the current signal strength of your phone, followed by the name of your cell phone provider (or, if you're roaming, who you're roaming with). The next icon over shows the strength of the wireless Internet network you're connected to (if you're in an area with an open high-speed wireless network, your iPhone lets you jump on that network. If you've got a high-speed wireless connection at home or the office, it jumps on that Wi-Fi network and your email and webpages load faster than a greased pig. If not, it uses either a 3G net-work or your carrier's EDGE network as your connection—you'll see a small 3G or E icon up top—which is somewhat slower, but not as slow as dial-up. Nothing is as slow as dial-up. Glaciers form faster than dial-up). If you see the icon of an airplane up there, you're in Airplane mode, which means your phone, bluetooth, and Internet connections are turned off (see Chapter 11 for more on Airplane mode, which you generally only use on airplanes or if you're seriously freaky about conserving battery power). If you're playing music on your iPhone, you'll see a mini Play button up there, and if you've got an alarm set (using the Clock func-tion), then you'll see a mini clock icon. If you see a blue or white Bluetooth icon up there, it means your iPhone is connected to a Bluetooth device (like a wireless headset or Bluetooth car connection). If the Bluetooth logo is gray, Bluetooth is on, but nothing's connected. You can pretty much figure what the battery icon is for (if not, see the next page).

Finding Out How Much Battery Time Is Left

At the top-right corner of your iPhone's touchscreen is a little battery charge indicator icon. If it's solid white, you're fully charged. If it's half-filled, so is your battery. If you get low on battery power, don't worry—your iPhone will let you know. A message will appear when you're down to just a 20% battery charge, and then it will warn you again when it gets to a 10% charge. When you plug your iPhone into your computer or AC adapter to charge your iPhone, a really huge battery icon appears onscreen (it doesn't really appear—it dominates your screen), so you can see the current battery charge status from across the room.

---

iTip

If you're charging your iPhone, your battery charge icon (up in the top-right corner of your screen) will have a lightning bolt on it. If your battery is fully charged, it displays a power plug graphic on the battery icon instead.

Using the Built-In Keyboard

Anytime you need to type something on your iPhone, a keyboard automatically appears onscreen. If the keys look kind of small, that's only because they are. Luckily, Apple has some features that make using the keyboard a lot easier. As you type onscreen, a large version of the letter you just typed pops up in front of your finger so you can see instantly if you hit the right letter. I can tell you from experience that the more you use this keyboard, the easier it gets, so if you wind up misspelling just about every word when you first start, don't sweat it—in just a couple of days, you'll be misspelling only every third or fourth word. There's also a pretty clever auto-complete function. Although it will suggest a word while you're typing it, go ahead and finish the word (especially if you've spelled it wrong) and it will replace your misspelled word with the correct word (95% of the time). You do have to get used to typing a word, seeing that you've misspelled it, and continuing to type. If you do that, you'll be amazed at how quickly you'll be able to type using this keyboard.

iTip

If you need to go back and fix a typo that the auto-complete feature didn't catch, just press-and-hold approximately where the typo occured and a magnifying Loupe appears onscreen so you can not only clearly see the location of your cursor, but you can move the cursor with your finger, as well, to quickly let you fix the mistake.

Using iPhone's Touchscreen to Navigate

The touchscreen on your iPhone's high-resolution screen works amazingly well, and there are just a few little techniques to learn so you're not only very accurate when using it, but have fun as well. Here are the three biggies:

(1) Don't press too hard. It just takes a light tap on the touchscreen to activate any button or select any item.

(2) Aim your finger either at the center of the button or object you want to select, or just above the center. If you aim any lower, you'll probably select the object below what you are trying to select.

(3) To scroll on the touchscreen, or move an object (like a slider), you touch the screen lightly and just "swipe" from left to right across the screen (Apple calls this "flicking," but it feels more like a swipe to me). For example, to see the album art in your iPhone's iPod, just touch an album lightly with your finger and slide it over to the left (or right). You don't have to slide very far at all—plus, you can just kind of flick it to scroll or move faster. (Oh, now I get that whole "flicking" thing.)

Syncing Your iPhone

"Syncing your iPhone" just means you're connecting your iPhone to your computer (your Mac or PC) and syncing the songs, videos, contacts, calendars, etc., between the two. This happens automatically when you connect your iPhone to your computer. When your computer detects your iPhone, it launches iTunes and starts syncing your content automatically (if you have this preference set). However, you can set preferences for exactly what gets uploaded to your iPhone. You do this in iTunes once your iPhone is connected to your computer. Simply click on your iPhone in the Devices list on the left side of the iTunes window and your iPhone preferences appear in the main iTunes window (as seen here). There are individual tabs for music, video, photos, info (calendar, contacts, etc.), ringtones, podcasts, and applications. For example, click on the Music tab, and the iPhone music preferences appear, where you can choose which playlists get uploaded or if all of your playlists and songs get transferred to your iPhone.

---

iTip

If you add a contact to your Contacts list from right within your iPhone, the next time you sync up with your computer, it adds that contact to your computer's contact list, so both your iPhone and your computer stay "in sync." It's a "no strings attached" type of arrangement. (Did anybody get that vague *NSYNC reference? My 11-year-old did.)

Using the Apple Headset (Headphones)

TERRY WHITE

If you're going to listen to music, or videos, or audiobooks, or…well, you get the idea, you're going to want to use the stereo headset that comes with your iPhone. It plugs right into the special headset jack at the top of the iPhone. Here's why Apple calls it a "headset" rather than "headphones": if you're listening to something on the iPhone and a call comes in, you can pause the music (or video) and take the call by pressing a tiny button attached to the headset's cord (shown circled above). You don't have to pick up the phone to talk, because there's a tiny mic built into that button, which hangs on the cord right where it needs to be for you to carry on a normal conversation. (By the way, you can also use this button on the cord to switch music tracks when you're listening to your iPhone's iPod.)

Using the Headset's Button

SCOTT KELBY

So you may be wondering, "If the button on your headset cord lets you pause the music to answer a call or skip to the next song, how does it know whether you want it to pause or skip to the next song?" Great question (wish I'd thought of it myself). To pause the music, you just click the button once. To skip to the next song, you click two times in quick succession (a double-click, if you will). But it does even more than that (this is one smart button for being so darn small). For example, if you're on one call and you get another call coming in (via call waiting), you can click once to hold the current call and jump over and take the incoming call. If you want the incoming call to go straight to your voicemail instead, then just click-and-hold the button for a few seconds and when you let go, off it goes. Okay, last scenario: you're on one call and another call comes in, and you want to hang up from your first call and take this new call. You click-and-hold the button for a couple of seconds until you hear two little beeps, which lets you know that you've hung up with caller #1, and you're now on with caller #2, the winner of a call-waiting standoff.

Zooming In for a Better View

A cool feature of the touchscreen is the ability to zoom your view in tighter on webpages, emails, or in the Maps feature. You do this by either: (1) double-tapping on the area you want to zoom in to (let's say you're on a webpage and you want to zoom in to read an article. Just double-tap right on that area [it's like double-clicking with a mouse—just two quick taps], and it zooms in). Or, the second method (2) is to "pinch out," which is where you pinch your index finger and thumb together (like you're pinching something), and then you touch the screen with these two fingers pinched together and quickly spread them out. As you spread out your fingers, the screen zooms in (again, this only works on webpages, email, and the Maps feature, so if you're trying this on the All Contacts list, you're going to get really frustrated). To zoom back out, start with your fingers apart— touch the top of the screen with your index finger and the bottom with your thumb— and pinch inward until they touch (like you're trying to pinch the screen).

---

iTip

Here's a tip we learned from our friend, author David Pogue: the secret to quickly adding any punctuation is to tap-and-hold on the punctuation button, and in a moment the punctuation characters will appear. Now just slide your finger over to the character you want and then remove your finger. It immediately returns you to the regular alphabetical keyboard. Thanks for sharing that one David—we use it every single day!

Turning on Silent Mode

Stepping into a meeting? About to testify in court? Going to a meeting about your upcoming testimony in court? Then you might want to switch your iPhone to Silent mode so you're not interrupted by any errant sounds, alarms, or ringtones during the sentencing phase of your trial. You do this by moving the Ring/Silent switch (found on the top-left side of your iPhone, and circled here in red) to Silent mode (which has you moving the switch toward the back of the iPhone. Don't worry—you'll see a large icon appear onscreen to indicate which mode you've just switched to). If your case is dismissed, you can switch back to regular Ring mode by moving the Ring/Silent switch back towards the screen side of your iPhone.

When the iPhone Rings

When you hear your iPhone ring, that's a pretty good indication that someone's calling you (I'm sorry—I just couldn't resist). When you do get a call, your iPhone displays the number of the person who's calling (or it displays their name if they're already in your All Contacts list). Now, if your iPhone is sleeping (it's been in your pocket, or your purse, etc.), you can answer the call by dragging the green Slide to Answer button to the right. To ignore the call (and have it go straight to your voicemail), just press the Sleep/Wake button (once) at the top of the iPhone, which also silences the ring. If a call comes in while your iPhone is wide awake (for example, you're not on the phone, but you're using another part of the iPhone, like checking your email or checking out a website), then two buttons will appear at the bottom of the screen: To accept the call, press the green Answer button. To decline the call (and send it straight into your voicemail), press the red Decline button (doing this also immediately silences the ring).

iPhone Accessories & Third-Party Applications

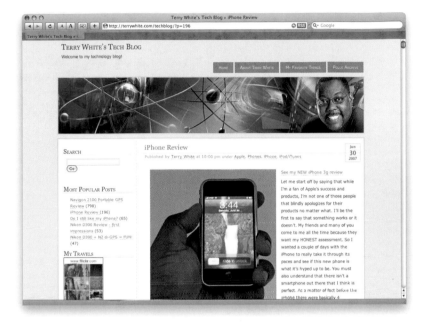

There are new accessories coming out daily for the iPhone. Our favorites to date are the DLO HipCase for iPhone, which is a side holster-style case for the iPhone, and the Griffin Technology PowerJolt for iPhone, which allows you to charge your iPhone in your car (other adapters work, too). However, since there will be so many accessories that come out after this book goes to press, we thought we'd give you a bonus by being able to check out our favorite accessories for the iPhone online anytime. Check www.scottkelby.com/iphonegear or http://terrywhite.com/techblog for the latest iPhone accessory reviews.

Chapter Two
Phoneheads
How to Use the iPhone's Phone

 I thought "Phoneheads" was a great name for this chapter, but it's not the name of a song; it's the name of a band that plays electronic music, which is why you probably haven't heard of them. My guess is that you don't listen to much electronic music. I'm not talking about music made with electronics (like electric guitars or synths), I'm talking about the kind of music you hear your teenagers playing, and you shake your head in disgust telling them, "That's not music!" Then one day, when you hear Van Halen's "Jamie's Cryin'" playing on your oldies station, you look in your rear view mirror and tell your kids, "Now that's music!" The sad thing is—you're right. That was music. And the stuff kids are listening to today is nothing more than an aural assault on everything we hold sacred about "real" music, which includes: white headbands, skinny ties, parachute pants, big hair, the hood of Whitesnake's car, inexpensive gas, and cassette tapes. Now *that* was music. I'm pretty safe in saying all this because you bought an iPhone, which means you must be pretty well off (or just incredibly loose with money), because iPhones aren't cheap. That means you're probably in your late 30s or early 40s, and you think that electronic music isn't music, so when I wrote that earlier, you were nodding your head. But, there is a second scenario: one in which you're young, and have rich parents, and they bought you an iPhone because they're loose with money. In that case, make sure you check out Phonehead's track "Syrinx (TGM Mix)." I love that song!

Importing Contacts from Your Computer

If you're a Macintosh user, there are four contact manager applications that let you sync directly from your computer to your iPhone, and they are: (1) your Mac's Address Book application (shown above), (2) Microsoft Entourage (see Chapter 10 for how to set this up), (3) Yahoo! Address Book, or (4) Google Contacts. If your contacts are in any one of those four, when you plug your iPhone into your computer, it launches iTunes and syncs the contacts on your computer with your iPhone (if you have this preference set). Or, you can click on the Info preferences tab in the main iTunes window, and choose which contacts to sync. If you're working on a corporate Microsoft Exchange Server, see your IT department for the proper configuration settings. If you have a MobileMe (.Mac) account, you can configure your iPhone to sync from within your computer's System Preferences.

If you're a Windows user, it works pretty much the same way, but the four contact managers it supports direct importing from are: (1) Yahoo! Address Book, (2) Windows Contacts, (3) Microsoft Outlook, and (4) Google Contacts. Of course, if you're a corporate user on a Microsoft Exchange server, you can get your contacts over the air, as well. Again, see your IT department for the settings. If you have a MobileMe account, you can configure your settings from within your computer's MobileMe Preferences, found in your Control Panel in the network preferences.

Importing Contacts from Your Old Phone

Okay, this gets a little stickier (well, at least stickier than what we did on the previous page, which was import contacts already on your computer in a contact manager). So, here's the thing: what you have to do is (you knew this was coming, right?) get the contacts in your old phone onto your computer. Then you can go back to the previous page and follow those instructions. On a Mac, there's a utility program called iSync (made by Apple and already installed on every Macintosh made in the past few years) that does the syncing from your phone to your computer for you, and it imports your contact info into Apple's own Address Book application (which syncs with your iPhone, no sweat). If your old phone isn't compatible with iSync or you're on a Windows PC, you can use a utility called The Missing Sync for iPhone by Mark/Space (http://markspace.com/missingsync_iphone.php). Again, once you get your contacts on your computer, then follow the instructions on the previous page.

Dialing Using the Standard Keypad

If you want to dial a number, you can just type in the number (like you would on any other phone) by tapping once on the Phone button, then tapping on the Keypad button to bring up the standard phone dialing buttons you see above. To dial a number, just tap the number keys. If you make a mistake, press the Back button (the button to the right of the green Call button) to erase that digit.

---

iTip

If you want to redial the last number you manually dialed, in the Phone app, tap the Keypad button and then tap Call. This will display the last number you dialed manually and tapping Call again will actually dial it.

Saving a Dialed Number as a Contact

If you've just entered a number using the keypad, and you realize you'd like to add it as a contact (so you can dial it again in the future with just one tap), then once the full number appears at the top of the Keypad screen (as seen here), tap the Add Contact button (which appears to the immediate left of the green Call button). This brings up a dialog asking if you want to save this as a new contact, or if you want to add this number to an existing contact.

Manually Adding Contacts

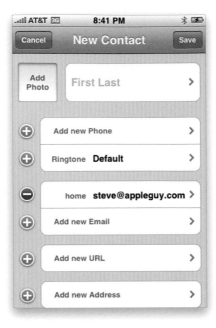

If you want to add a contact manually (by manually, I mean just typing it right into your iPhone), just tap on the Phone button, then tap on the Contacts button, then tap the + (plus sign) button in the upper right-hand corner. This brings up a New Contact screen, and to add some contact info, just tap on the info you want to add (for example, to add your new contact's email address, just tap on Add New Email and a screen appears ready for you to type in their email address on the keyboard at the bottom of the screen). When you're done entering the email address, tap the Save button in the top-right corner of that screen, and you return to the New Contact screen to add more info the same way.

---

iTip

Here's a tip to help you think like your iPhone: most of the time, if you see a button in the upper-left corner of the screen, it acts like a Back button in a Web browser—pressing it will take you back to the previous screen you were on.

Dialing Someone in Your Contacts List

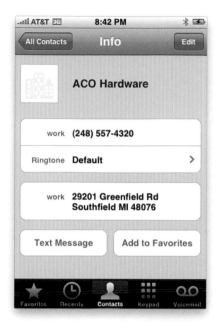

To dial someone in your Contacts list, tap on the Phone button, then tap on the Contacts button (okay, that was pretty obvious), and then tap on the person's name in the list. This brings up their full contact info, including a list of all their phone numbers you have added (cell number, home, office, etc.). To dial one of those numbers, just tap once on it and it starts dialing.

 iTip

When you're in the All Contacts list, if you want to jump directly to a particular letter quickly, just tap once on the letter in the alphabetic list on the far-right side of the screen. You can also tap, hold, and slide up/down the list, as well.

Seeing Each Contact's Photo When They Call

How would you like for each contact's photo to appear when they call you? (It's great for seeing who's calling at just a glance—without having to read their name or figure out who it is.) There are two ways to do this: (1) use a photo already on your iPhone, or (2) take a photo using the iPhone's built-in camera and use that photo. Start at the Home screen, then tap the Phone button, then the Contacts button. Scroll to the contact you want to assign a photo to, tap their name, then tap the Edit button in the top-right corner of the screen. In the upper-left corner of the Info screen, tap on Add Photo. This brings up two new buttons: Take Photo (so you can take a photo of your contact using the iPhone's built-in camera), and Choose Existing Photo (which lets you choose any photo you've already imported into your iPhone). Tap whichever one you want. If you tapped the Choose Existing Photo button, it takes you to your Photo Albums screen, where you can tap on the photo you want to assign to your contact. This brings you to a screen where you can determine the size and position of the photo that will display when your contact calls (use your finger to slide it around, which basically crops the photo, or "pinch it" with your fingers to scale it up or down). When it looks good to you, tap the gray Set Photo button and you're done. If, instead, you tapped the Take Photo button, just take the photo, scale and move it, and tap Set Photo. This is cool, but the picture won't be in the Camera Roll for download later. So if it's a picture you will want to use for other purposes, take the picture first and add it to the contact afterwards.

Shooting a Photo and Adding It to a Contact

If you want to take a photo using your iPhone's built-in camera and add it to an existing contact, start at the Home screen, then tap on the Camera button. Aim the camera and take a photo of your contact by tapping the camera shutter button at the bottom center of the screen. You'll hear the shutter sound to let you know the photo has been taken, but to see the photo you just took, you have to tap the stacked photos button that appears to the left of the camera shutter button. This brings up the Camera Roll screen, where you'll see little thumbnails of the photos you've taken. Tap the photo you want to assign, and it will appear full screen. Now, a row of buttons appears along the bottom of the screen. Tap the button on the far left and a pop-up menu will appear. To assign this photo to a contact, tap the Assign to Contact button, and it brings up your All Contacts list. Tap on the contact you want to assign that photo to, and it shows you a preview of how the final photo is going to look when the contact calls, so you can move and scale it the way you want (using your finger to slide the photo around onscreen, which basically crops the photo to your liking, or "pinching it" with your fingers to scale it up or down). When it looks good to you, press the gray Set Photo button and you're done.

Turn a Recent Caller into a Contact

If someone has just called you that isn't in your All Contacts list (but you'd like to add them as a contact), start at the Home screen, tap on the Phone button, then tap on Recents. Scroll to the number of the person you want to add as a contact, then tap on the button with the arrow in the blue circle to the right of their number. This brings up an info screen, and near the bottom of this screen you'll see a button called Create New Contact. Tap that button and the New Contact screen appears with their phone number already entered for you—you just have to type in their name, address, etc. When you're done, tap the Save button in the upper-right corner of the screen.

iTip

If you'd like to add a note to a contact (like a description of who this person is, or how you know them), tap on the contact, and when their Info screen appears, tap on the Edit button (in the top-right corner). Then in the Info edit screen that appears, scroll down and tap on Add Field, then scroll down and tap on Note to add a Note field. This brings up the Edit Note screen, where you can type in your note using the keyboard that appears at the bottom of the screen.

Assigning Ringtones to Specific Callers

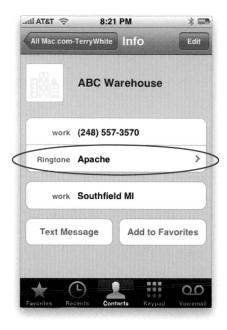

If you'd like to assign a ringtone to a specific caller (for example, I have a ringtone assigned to my wife's cell phone number, so I instantly know it's her without even looking at my phone), here's what to do: Start at the Home screen, then tap the green Phone button, then tap the Contacts button. Tap on the contact you want to assign a ringtone to, then when their Info screen appears, tap on Default (next to Ringtone), and you'll be taken to the Ringtones screen, with a list of all your ringtones. To assign a ringtone to this contact, just tap on one (it will play a sample of the ringtone when you tap on it). When you find the ringtone you want, just tap the blue Info button at the top left of the screen, and it returns you to the contact's Info screen, where you'll see the name of the ringtone you just assigned in the Ringtone field. Now when this contact calls, you'll hear their custom ringtone rather than the default ringtone that you'll hear when anyone else calls.

---

iTip

The iPhone can sync notes from your calendar entries and contacts. So if you have notes in another application that you want to sync from your computer, add them to your contacts or calendar entries to get them on the iPhone.

Search for a Contact

With the iPhone's version 2 software, Apple introduced the ability to search for contacts. When you go to your All Contacts list (from the Home screen, tap the Phone button, then tap Contacts), there will be a search field at the top the list. Tap in the search field to get the keyboard, start typing the name of the contact you're looking for, and the iPhone will immediately begin narrowing down the list to names that match what you've typed. Once you see the name you're looking for, you can stop typing and tap the contact you found to bring up their Info screen and make your call.

---

iTip

If you want to narrow the list down even further, type the first letter of the first name, then type a space, and then type the first letter of the last name. This will narrow the list down to only the contacts with those initials. You can still keep typing to get to the name you want. So if you wanted to find Scott Kelby, you'd type "S Kel" and that would narrow the list down quicker than having to scroll through multiple Scotts.

Adding a Pause

If you're calling an automated system that requires you to enter a series of numbers, such as an account number or extension and then a PIN, you can add those pauses and additional numbers directly to your contact's Info screen. From the Home screen, tap the Phone button, then tap on Contacts to bring up your All Contacts list. Tap on the contact that requires the additional string of numbers and pauses. Tap the Edit button in the top right of the screen, then tap on the phone number that you need to edit. Now, tap the symbol key (+*#) at the bottom left of the keyboard. This will change the 0 key to a Pause key. Now you can tap the Pause key to enter a two-second pause, and then enter the next string of numbers. If you need a longer pause, just continue to tap the Pause key for as many two-second pauses as you need. Once you're done, tap Save at the top right of the screen to save the number and then tap Done to save the contact's changes. The next time you need to log into that system, just bring up that contact and tap the number. The iPhone will dial the complete string, with pauses and all.

The iPhone's Version of Speed Dial

The iPhone's name for speed dial is "Favorites," and to turn one of your contacts into a Favorite, just tap on their name in your All Contacts list to view the screen with their full contact info. Then, in the bottom-right corner of their Info screen, tap on the Add to Favorites button (shown circled here in red), and that contact is added to your Favorites screen. Now, there is another way to do it, and that is to start at the Favorites screen (you tap the Favorites button), then tap the little + (plus sign) button in the upper-right corner. This brings up your All Contacts list, and you just tap on the name of the contact you want added to your Favorites. If your contact has only one phone number (like just a home number, or just a cell number), they're immediately added as a Favorite. If they have multiple numbers, then it brings up all their numbers and you just tap on the number you want added as a Favorite.

Removing a Favorite

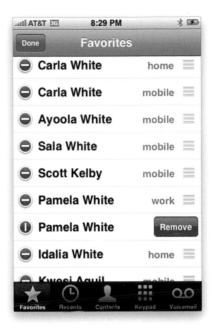

If you decide that someone's not your Favorite anymore (hey, it happens), you can easily remove them. Just tap the Edit button in the top-left corner of the Favorites screen, and a red circle with a − (minus sign) will appear before each Favorite. To remove a Favorite from your list, just tap directly on its red minus button, and a red Remove button will appear to its right (as seen above). Tap that Remove button and it's gone!

Reordering Your Favorites

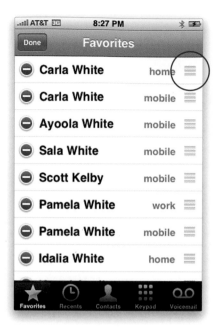

If you don't like the order you added your Favorites in, you can reorder them. Just tap on the Edit button, and then on the far right of each contact, just past the type of phone number (mobile, home, etc.), you'll see three short horizontal lines (circled in red above). Now, you're going to drag your contacts into the order you want them by tapping-and-holding on those lines and dragging your contact up (or down) until they're in the order you want them (it's easier than it sounds).

Seeing the Contact Info for a Favorite

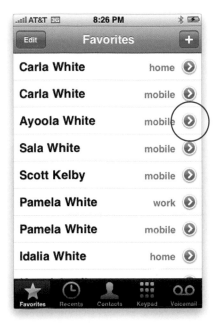

To see the full contact info for any of your Favorites, just tap once on the little blue circle with a right-facing arrow that appears to the right of the contact (shown circled above), and the full Info screen appears for that contact.

The Advantage of Contact Groups

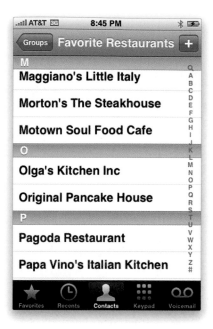

If the contact manager on your computer allows you to have caller groups, this can make getting to the contacts you want much easier. For example, you could have a group for your favorite restaurants, and one just for your friends, and one for your co-workers, and…well, you get the idea. That way, when you go to the All Contacts screen, you can tap the Groups button (in the upper-left corner) to see a list of your different groups. Then, you can tap on a group and see just those contacts (like seeing just your favorite restaurants, as shown above).

How to Know If You Missed Any Calls

If you miss a call, you'll see the caller's name and Missed Call onscreen when you wake your iPhone from sleep (well, you'll see their name if they're in your Contacts list. If they're not, you'll just see their number and Missed Call). If you missed a call, when you press the Home button, you'll see the green Phone button now has a small red circle on its top-right corner with the number of calls you missed. Okay, here's where it gets a little weird: that number is not actually the number of calls you've missed, it's the calls you've missed combined with the number of unheard phone messages you've been left. So, if you missed five calls but those five callers all left messages, then you'll see the number 10, which represents those five missed calls and five voicemail messages, even though only five people actually called. I told you it was weird.

Returning Missed Calls

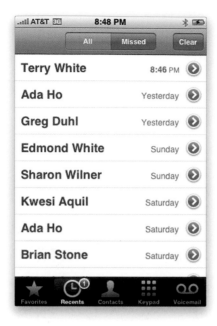

To return a missed call, on the Home screen, tap the green Phone button, then tap the Recents button at the bottom of the screen. This brings up a list of all recent calls, and the calls you see listed in red are your missed calls. To see only your missed calls, tap the Missed button at the top. To return a missed call, just tap on it and it dials that number. (*Note:* The number of missed calls appears in a small red circle in the top-right corner of the Recents button.)

---

iTip

To clear any missed calls and your list of recent calls, go to the Recents screen and tap the Clear button in the top-right corner of the screen.

Seeing If You Have Messages

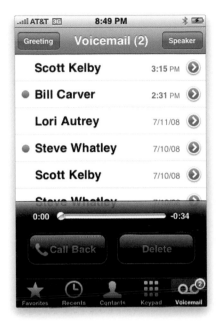

If a caller left you a voicemail message, you'll see the caller's name (if they're in your Contacts list—if not, their phone number) when you wake your iPhone from sleep. When you tap the green Phone button, you'll see the Voicemail button, and on it you'll see a red circle displaying the number of messages you have waiting. To see a list of your voicemails (yes, you see a list—that's why Apple calls this "Visual Voicemail"), tap on the Voicemail button, and you'll see a list of the contacts (or numbers) who've left you a voicemail message, and when they called (as seen above). Messages with a round blue button before them haven't been listened to yet.

Deleting Heard Voicemails

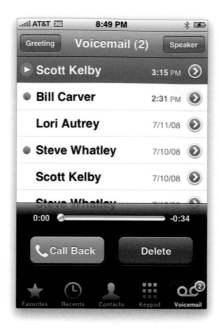

The beauty of this system is you don't have to listen to your messages in order—you can tap directly on the message you want to hear and that message plays (you'll have to hold the iPhone up to your ear to hear the message). To hear your messages through your iPhone's speaker, tap the Speaker button on the top right. You'll see a status bar that moves from left to right as your message plays, which gives you a visual cue as to how long the message actually is. Now, here's the thing: when a message is new, you just tap on it and it plays. But once you've heard it, the rules change—now to hear a voicemail, you tap on the message you want to hear, and a little blue Play/Pause button appears before that message. To hear the message again, tap that little blue button. To pause the message, tap that same little blue button again. To return a call, tap on the message, then tap the green Call Back button. To delete a message, tap on it, then tap on the red Delete button. Once you delete a message, it's not really deleted from your iPhone—it just moves that message to a deleted area (kind of the way deleting a file on your computer just puts it in your Trash or Recycle Bin). You can still see, and hear, your deleted messages by tapping on (I know—it's pretty obvious) Deleted Messages (at the end of your voicemail list). Once there, to move a deleted message back to your regular list, just tap on it, then tap the gray Undelete button. However, if you really want this voicemail off your iPhone for good, tap on the message and tap the Clear All button.

Replay Just Part of a Message

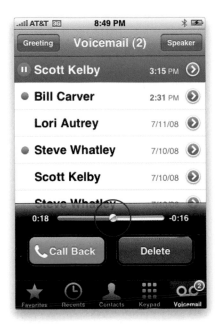

This is an iPhone feature I just love: while your message is playing, you can grab the little slider and "scrub" back a few seconds and hear anything you just missed—in real time. So, for example, let's say you're listening to a message and the person on the message gives you a phone number. To hear that phone number again (without having to listen to the entire message again), you can just tap-and-hold on the little status bar knob and drag it back a little bit (just like you would scrub through a video), and hear it again. Yes, other phones can do something similar, but because you're dragging the audio live, you can quickly drag right to the spot you want to hear again. Try it once, and you'll see the difference it makes.

Putting a Call on Hold to Call Someone Else

If you're on a call and need to make another call, you can put that call on hold and make a different call (kind of like having a two-line phone). Just tap the Hold button on the touchscreen, then tap the Add Call button. This brings up your All Contacts list, and you can tap on a name to dial that contact, or you can just dial a number by tapping on the Keypad button that appears in the bottom-right corner of the All Contacts screen. If you want to switch back to your original call, you can just tap the Swap button.

Recording Your Outgoing Message

By default, you get a generic "I'm not here, man" voicemail message, but creating your own custom message is just too easy to continue using that default message. Just tap on the Voicemail button, then in the top-left corner of the Voicemail screen, tap on the Greeting button to bring up the Greeting screen. You'll see two choices: (a) Default (the generic pre-recorded greeting), and (b) Custom (where you create your own). Tap on Custom, and Play and Record buttons appear at the bottom of the screen. Tap the white Record button, hold the iPhone up to your ear (like you are answering a call), and just say your message into it. When you're done, tap the red Stop button, and to hear it, tap the blue Play button. If you don't like your message, just tap the white Record button again and record a new message. When it sounds good to you, tap the Save button in the upper-right corner of the screen.

---

 iTip

Don't sing messages into your iPhone, as a sensor was designed by Apple to detect really bad singing and when it analyzes your voice and determines that it is indeed bad singing, it automatically forwards your message, along with a picture of you, to YouTube where it's then featured in a public humiliation forum. Well, at least that's what I've been told.

Sending Text Messages (SMS)

There are two ways to send text messages from your iPhone: From the Home screen, (1) tap directly on the green SMS Text button (upper-left corner), which brings up the Text Messages screen. In the upper-right corner, there's a button that is a square icon with a pen in it—tap on that button and the New Message screen appears, where you enter your contact's name (or phone number if they're not in your Contacts list), and then type in your message using the keyboard (if you want to choose a contact from your Contacts list, just tap on the + [plus sign] button to the right of the To field and your All Contacts list will appear). Or (2) you can tap the Phone button, tap on the Contacts button, and tap on any contact. Once their contact info appears, tap the Text Message button (it's below all their contact info). This brings up the same New Message screen, where you compose your text message. When you're done entering your message, just tap the Send button and your message is sent.

Sending Text Messages to Multiple People

It is possible to send the same SMS text message to two or more people at once. When you launch the SMS Text app, you can type in the name of the first person (or phone number if they are not in your Contacts list), tap out of the To field, tap back into the To field, then continue typing in another name or number for another person you want to text, etc. You can also tap the + (plus sign) button to add contacts directly from your All Contacts list.

 iTip

When you're typing a message, don't sweat little misspellings, as the iPhone will normally catch them and fix them for you. Just keep typing and watch how it cleans up after you and fixes the spelling of the words. It takes a little getting used to—typing and letting the typos stand—but give it a try and you'll be amazed at how well it works.

Reading Text Messages

If you've received a text message, you'll see the name of the person who sent it (if they're in your Contacts list) and the first two lines of their message as soon as you wake the iPhone from sleep. Unlocking it will take you directly to the message. If you are using your iPhone, when you go to the Home screen, you'll now see a little red circle added to the top right of the green SMS Text button with the number of unread text messages you have waiting. Tap on that SMS Text button and you'll see your new message. To see a list of all your text messages, tap on the Messages button in the upper-left corner. To see any message in the list, just tap on it. Now it gets fun: if you are texting back and forth, you'll see your text conversation appear in "talk bubbles" (as seen above). Your messages appear in a green bubble, replies appear in a gray bubble, and visually it looks like you're having a conversation (if you're a Macintosh user, you'll probably recognize this, as it looks just like Apple's iChat online chat software that comes on all Macs).

---

iTip

When you receive an SMS text message, your iPhone will sound an alert (provided you have that preference set in your Sounds settings). However, you may be away from your phone or unable to hear it in a noisy environment, so it will sound up to two more times (about three minutes apart) to remind you that you have a message waiting.

Muting Your Call/Hearing Through Speaker

If you're on a call and don't want the caller to hear what you're saying for a moment, tap the Mute button on the touchscreen. When you're ready to start talking again, tap the Mute button again. If you have a call in progress and want to hear your conversation through the iPhone's speaker, tap the Speaker button on the touchscreen.

Making Instant Conference Calls

This is another one of those features that will make you fall in love with your iPhone. To add another person to your call in progress (for a three-way call), just tap the Add Call button on the touchscreen, and it brings up your All Contacts list. Tap the contact's name you want added to your three-way call, and it dials them. Now tap the Merge Calls button to add them to your existing conversation. If the person you want added to your call isn't in your All Contacts list, then you can dial them by tapping once on the Keypad button in the bottom-right corner of the All Contacts screen.

Dialing an Extension

So, let's say you dial a number and you get one of those "If you know your party's extension, please dial it now" greetings. I know—how hard could it be? Actually, it's easy—if you know how. All you have to do is tap the Keypad button on your touchscreen, and then dial the extension. I know, it sounds really easy now, but I've seen people totally stumped when it happens to them.

Check Your Email While You're On the Phone

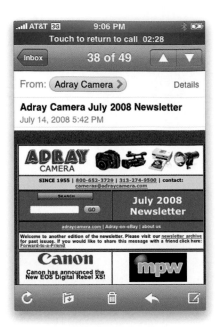

If you're in a really boring phone conversation, do what everybody else in the business world does—check your email. It makes things easier if you start by tapping the Speaker button (so you can still hear your conversation while you're looking at the touchscreen). Then press the Home button, then tap the Mail button. Don't worry—your call will stay live even though you're doing something completely different. However, there's always a chance that the person you're talking with will also become bored, and start checking their email, too. It's a chance you have to take. Anyway, to return to your call screen, just tap once at the very top of your screen (where it says Touch to Return to Call), and it takes you back there. *Note:* Checking your email or surfing the Web while on the phone is not supported over most EDGE networks.

Pausing the Music to Take a Call

SCOTT KELBY

If you've got your headset (earbuds) on and you're listening to music and a phone call comes in, you can pause the song and jump over to take the call all in one click (that's right—it's a click, not a tap). There's a little tiny button attached to the earbuds (about 10" from the right earbud itself. It doesn't look like a button, it looks like a thin little plastic rectangle). Click that button, and the song playing is paused, and it answers your call. When you're done with the call, click the button again to hang up and pick up the song right where you left off.

Ignoring an Incoming Call

If a call comes in, and you can't take the call right then, but don't want the phone to continue ringing, then just press the Sleep/Wake button on the top of the iPhone. This stops the ringing and sends the call into your voicemail.

Turning the Ringer Off

If you don't want to hear your iPhone's ringer at all, press the Home button, then tap on the Settings button. When the Settings screen shows up, tap on Sounds, then in the Ring section, tap-and-drag the Ring volume slider (it's directly below the Vibrate setting) all the way to the left. This turns your ring volume off. By default, your phone will still vibrate when a call comes in, but there won't be an audible ring. If you want to turn that vibration off as well, in the Ring section, switch the Vibrate control to the OFF setting by tapping once just to the right of the blue ON setting.

Choosing Your Ringtone

The default ringtone for your iPhone is a marimba sound, but if you'd like to change it, start at the Home screen, then tap on the Settings button. When the Settings screen appears, tap on Sounds, then under the Ring volume slider you'll see the Ringtone control. Tap on Ringtone, and it takes you to a screen listing all the built-in ringtones and any custom ringtones you've synced to your iPhone. You'll see a checkmark appear to the right of Marimba, indicating that it's the currently selected ringtone. To change your ringtone, tap on the name of the one you want. That ringtone plays (so you can hear if you really want to select it), and if you want to keep this new sound as your ringtone, just leave that screen (tap the Sounds button in the top-left corner of the Ringtone screen, or press the Home button).

Stop People You Call from Seeing Your Number

If you want to call somebody, but you'd prefer that they not see your iPhone's number, you can turn off the feature that shares your number with whomever you call. To do that, start at the Home screen, then tap on the Settings button. When the Settings screen appears, scroll down and tap on Phone. When the Phone settings screen appears, scroll down and you'll find a control called Show My Caller ID. To keep your number private, tap on that control and it brings up the Show My Caller ID screen with an ON/OFF button. Now tap to the immediate right of the blue ON setting to switch this feature off.

Setting Up Call Forwarding

To have calls coming into your iPhone forwarded to another phone, start at the Home screen, then tap on the Settings button. When the Settings screen appears, scroll down and tap on Phone. When the Phone settings screen appears, scroll down to Call Forwarding. Tap on Call Forwarding to bring up the Call Forwarding screen. You'll see an ON/OFF button (and by default, Call Forwarding is set to OFF). To turn it on, tap once to the immediate left of the OFF setting. Now, you're probably wondering where your call is forwarded to. Once you turn on the Call Forwarding feature, if you don't already have a Forwarding To number entered, a screen where you enter the phone number to forward to will appear. Now, this next part throws a lot of people: there's no OK or Save button. You just have to tap the Call Forwarding button in the top-left corner and it returns you to the main Call Forwarding screen, where you'll see the number you just added and the ON setting. When you want to turn the Call Forwarding feature off, go back to the same screen (follow the steps above), and tap the ON setting and it will change to the OFF setting.

Using Apple's Bluetooth Wireless Headset

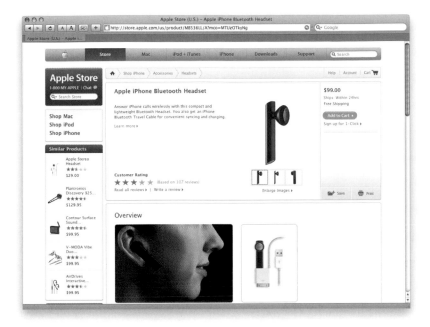

You can use the "hands-free" feature of your iPhone if you've bought either Apple's iPhone Bluetooth Headset, a third-party Bluetooth wireless headset, or if your car supports hands-free talking using its built-in Bluetooth feature, so your conversation happens through its stereo speakers and built-in mic (this feature is becoming more and more common in new cars). If you bought Apple's wireless Bluetooth headset, the setup is a breeze because it comes with a charging/syncing Dual Dock that holds your iPhone and your Apple wireless headset. You just plug the Dual Dock into your computer (or into a power outlet using the included charger), then put both your iPhone and your wireless headset in the Dual Dock, and it automatically syncs (called "autopairing") your iPhone to your wireless headset.

Other Headsets or Bluetooth in Your Car

If you have a third-party Bluetooth wireless headset, or you want to pair your iPhone to your car's Bluetooth feature, here's what to do: First you have to put your headset (or your car's Bluetooth feature) in Discoverable mode, which means you put it in a mode where other Bluetooth devices can find it. How this is done is different for every headset or car make and model, so look at your headset's instruction manual (or your car's owner's manual) for how to make it "discoverable". Once it's discoverable, start at your iPhone's Home screen, then tap on the Settings button. In the Settings screen, tap on General, then tap on Bluetooth. When the Bluetooth screen appears, tap to the immediate left of OFF to turn your iPhone's Bluetooth feature on. This starts your iPhone searching for any discoverable Bluetooth devices (like your wireless headset or your car's Bluetooth feature) that are within about 30 feet of where you are. Once it finds a Bluetooth device, it displays that device's name. Tap on the name, and in the next screen, enter the device's PIN (check the instructions that come with your headset or car kit for how to find this information). Tap the Connect button and they are paired (luckily, you only have to go through this process the first time. After that, it automatically recognizes your headset, or car).

Chapter Three

Please
Mr. Postman

Getting (and Sending)
Email on Your iPhone

 This is an incredibly important chapter, because email is incredibly important. If it weren't for the iPhone's ability to get email, I would have missed an amazing adventure. It all started with a desperate email from a Mr. Mabutuu, who (according to the email) had been a high-ranking government official in the small African nation of Nantango. I soon learned of the overthrow of his small, friendly government through a military coup that nearly cost him his life. He was able to flee to the safety of a small village protected by freedom fighters loyal to his ousted government, but before he fled the capital, he was able to move nearly $16 million of his government's surplus cash (in U.S. funds) to a small bank in a neighboring country. His main concern was that these funds not fall into the hands of the corrupt general who led the rebellion against him, and he asked if I would be so kind as to help him find a suitable U.S. bank where he could wire the $16 million. For my small role in providing my bank account number, username, password, and social security number, he would gladly share the $16 million with me rather than see it seized by the new hostile government (he proposed a 60/40 split, but I was able to negotiate it to 50/50). However, he was in a bind because before his bank would transfer the funds to my bank account, he would have to first pay $22,800 for the required doc stamps and tariffs to complete the wire transfer. Of course, I immediately wired the $22,800 to his overseas account, and since then, each day I patiently check my account for the transfer of the $16 million to hit (that's going to be a pretty exciting day for us both, eh?).

Setting Up Your Email (POP, IMAP, or Yahoo)

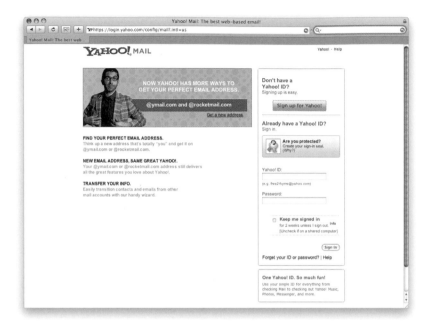

The iPhone supports the most common email standards. Luckily, if your email is already set up on your computer, then you'll have the option in iTunes to choose which email accounts you want to have working on your iPhone. If you don't have an email account yet or prefer not to use your existing email accounts, you can set up a free one on services like Yahoo.com, Google.com, or AOL.com. If you can't decide, I highly recommend using a free account on Yahoo.com. Why? Because setting up an account at www.mail .yahoo.com will give you free "push" type email for your iPhone. This means that instead of having to check for new messages, the emails will come to the phone automatically. All other types of accounts will need to be checked, which the iPhone can do automatically at regular intervals. The iPhone software (version 2) also has Microsoft Exchange Active Sync support (check with your company's IT department to get configuration info first).

---

iTip

If you have a choice between POP- or IMAP-based email, choose IMAP. The reason is that IMAP email resides on a server. When you read an email on your iPhone, it will be marked as read on the server so that when you go to your computer to check email, you won't have to read the ones you've already read. Same goes for trashing an email. Once trashed on the iPhone, it will be trashed on your computer, too.

Add an Email Account Right on the iPhone

If you choose not to have your email accounts synced from your computer through iTunes, you can add them directly on the iPhone. To do this, you'll need to know some things first. You'll need to know your:

- email address: you@somewhere.com
- email server type: POP, IMAP, or Exchange
- incoming server address (a.k.a. POP server): mail.domain.com
- outgoing server address (a.k.a. SMTP server): smtp.domain.com

Also, most outgoing mail servers require some kind of authentication for sending mail out when you're not on their network. You'll need to check with your ISP to find out what settings to use. Most ISPs display this info in the help section of their websites. When you set up your account, you probably received an email with all of this info.

Once you have this info, tap the Settings button on the iPhone and go to Mail, then under Accounts, tap Add Account. What's nice is that if your email account is on Microsoft Exchange, Apple's MobileMe, Google (Gmail), Yahoo, or AOL, the iPhone will know most of the geeky settings. All you'll need is your account info. If your account is not on one of these services, then tap Other and you'll have to key in the info that you gathered above.

Add a MobileMe Email Account

Apple has launched a new service called MobileMe, which offers direct push and syncing of your email similar to Microsoft Exchange. The cost of MobileMe is $99/year ($149/year for families). You can also sync your contacts and calendar to MobileMe and have this information wirelessly sync to your iPhone (requires iPhone version 2 software). MobileMe also includes an email account (.me) and when email is received on your MobileMe account, it is pushed out to your iPhone instantly. MobileMe is a cross-platform service for both Mac and Windows users. If you previously had a .Mac account, you now have a MobileMe account. Once you have your MobileMe account established, you can set up your iPhone to receive your MobileMe email by going to Settings, then to Mail, then tapping on Add Account, and tapping on MobileMe on the Add Account screen. Just enter your MobileMe account information, and you're all set.

Add a Corporate Microsoft Exchange Email Account

Apple has gone to great lengths to support corporate iPhone users. One of the most popular email servers used in corporate America is Microsoft's Exchange Server. Starting with iPhone version 2 software, you can now have direct push of email, calendar appointments, and contacts wirelessly, without having to sync via the USB cable to your computer. You'll have to first check with your corporate IT department to get the correct settings for your account. Once you have this information, just add a Microsoft Exchange account to your iPhone (from Settings, tap on Mail, then tap on Add Account, tap on Microsoft Exchange on the Add Account screen, and enter your Exchange account information). You'll get the option of whether or not you want your contacts and calendar synced, too. When email is received at your office, it is pushed out to your iPhone immediately. When someone proposes a meeting, you'll be able to respond and have the meeting added to your calendar instantly. Also, any changes to your contacts are automatically synced to the server. So you basically never have to sync this information via the USB cable. Don't throw the cable away just yet, though, you'll still need it to sync your iPhone for media, such as music and movies, as well as for iPhone software updates.

Checking Your Email

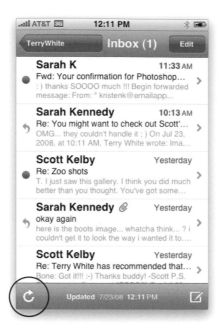

The iPhone is pretty smart in that there really isn't a check email button. It assumes that when you tap the Mail button on the Home screen, you probably want to check your email. At that time, it checks for new messages, provided you have either a Wi-Fi connection or connection to 3G or your carrier's EDGE data network. Once you're looking at your Inbox, you can also have the iPhone check for new mail immediately by tapping the curved arrow icon in the lower-left corner of the screen. The iPhone version 2 software offers the ability to either check for new email manually, on a schedule (such as every 30 minutes—just go to Settings, tap on Fetch New Data, and make your choice in the Fetch section), or if your email account supports it, via "push." For example, Microsoft Exchange and MobileMe email is automatically pushed out to your iPhone as soon as it comes in.

iTip

You can change your settings for Mail to automatically check for new messages every 15 minutes, every 30 minutes, or every hour. The more often the iPhone checks for email, the more it will use the battery. I chose every 30 minutes as a happy medium.

Reading Your Email

Once your email is set up and the messages start rolling in, they will be listed under the account that you set up. Unread messages will have a blue dot to the left of them. By default, the iPhone displays the first two lines of each message. You can then decide which emails you want to read in what order. When you want to display the entire email, just tap on the one you want to read and the email body will be displayed. You can scroll down the message by flicking your finger up on the screen. It's kind of counterintuitive at first because it's the opposite of the way you do it on your computer. Just think of flicking as the way you want the message to move. You want it to move up, so that you can read more of what's below. If the type is too small, you can use the pinch feature to zoom in and out: using two fingers on the display, such as your index finger and thumb, you spread them out to zoom in on the message, then pinch them in to zoom back out. You can also pan around the message by simply moving your finger around on the display in the direction you want the message to move. You can use the up and down arrows in the upper-right corner to navigate to the next message or previous message.

 iTip

You can mark a message that you are reading as unread by tapping the Details button in the upper-right corner of the message, then you will see a blue dot with Mark as Unread. Just tap this button and the message will stay marked as new.

Viewing Email Attachments

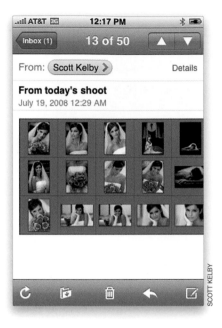

The iPhone supports viewing attachments such as JPGs, PDFs, Microsoft Office documents (Word, Excel, and PowerPoint), and iWork documents (Keynote, Numbers, and Pages). If you receive an image, such as a JPG, Mail does a great job showing the image right in the body of the message. If you receive one of the other file types in an email on your iPhone, the attachment will generally be at the bottom of the email message. Simply tap the attachment to view it. The iPhone will slide the message over to the left and show you the attachment in a separate screen. If you prefer to see the attachment in a horizontal view, just rotate your iPhone to the left or right. Once you're done viewing it, you can tap the Message button at the top of the screen to go back to the original email. If you have more than one attachment, you can view the next one once you return to the message.

 iTip

The fastest way to delete an email right in your Inbox (after you've read it, or if it's obviously spam, even before you read it) is to just swipe left to right over the message. This reveals a red Delete button, and to delete that email just tap on the button.

Adding Photo Attachments to Your Library

If you receive an email on your iPhone with a photo attached, you can add that photo to your iPhone's Camera Roll. Bring up your email by tapping the Mail button on the Home screen, and then tap on the email message containing the attached photo that you would like to add to your iPhone. Tap once directly on the image and a menu will pop up asking you to save it, so just tap on Save Image, and it will be added directly to your Camera Roll. You can see the image in the Camera Roll by pressing the Home button, then tapping the Photos button, and then tapping Camera Roll. Once you see the image, tap on it to see it full screen and then you can set it as a wallpaper picture, email it to others, send it to a MobileMe gallery (if you have a MobileMe account), or assign it to a contact by tapping on the image and then tapping on the little box with the arrow at the bottom left of the screen.

Dialing a Phone Number from an Email

You have to remember that the iPhone is a phone. Therefore, if someone sends you an email that contains a phone number, you can simply tap the phone number to dial it. The iPhone will automatically switch over to the Phone application and place the call. Once you're finished with your call, you can tap the End Call button. This will take you back to your email message.

iTip

The iPhone currently doesn't have a way to copy-and-paste a phone number from one application to the next. However, if you want to add a phone number to an existing contact or create a new contact with that phone number, tap the phone number you received in an email (or on a webpage in Safari) to dial it. Then tap End Call immediately. Now the call will show up in your Recents call list in the Phone application. From there, you can tap the right arrow to the right of the phone number and have the option to either Create New Contact or Add to Existing Contact.

Going to a Website from an Email Message

The iPhone does a great job of receiving HTML-style emails. The links in your email message, whether they are text links or links on images, are live. So tapping a link in an email will automatically fire up Safari (the Web browser application) and take you to the site that you tapped on in your email message. Once you're done browsing the site, you'll have to press the Home button and then tap the Mail button again to return to the message you were viewing.

iTip

Once you're in Safari and looking at the page you went to from the email message, you can bookmark it by tapping the + (plus sign) at the bottom of the screen. Once you add this bookmark, it will be automatically synced back to your computer the next time you sync your iPhone (if you have this preference set).

Replying to an Email Message

When you want to reply to a message, tap the arrow pointing to the left in the toolbar at the bottom of the email message (the second button from the right) and you will be presented with a pop-up menu. You will have a choice of Reply (Reply All if the message was sent to more than one person), Forward, or Cancel. When you tap Reply, you'll be presented with a new message already addressed to the original sender and with the original subject. The cursor will already be in the body and all you have to do is start typing your reply. If the original message was sent to you and other people, you can tap the Reply All button to send your reply to the original sender and all the people that the message was sent or copied to. Once you've typed your reply, simply hit the Send button in the upper-right corner. If you tap the Cancel button, you'll be prompted with the option to Save or Don't Save the message.

---

iTip

If you're on iPhone software version 2, you'll also see the new Bcc (blind carbon copy) field, and if you have multiple email addresses set up, you'll be able to choose which email address you want to send the reply from. Just tap in the Cc/Bcc, From field to activate the Cc and Bcc fields, and then tap in the From field to switch between email accounts for sending.

Filing an Email Message in a Folder

If you have an IMAP-based email account, it is possible to have additional folders on the server to store your messages in. You can move your iPhone email into any of these folders, as well. Since IMAP account folders reside on a server, the next time you check email on your computer or the webmail interface that your ISP provides, the mail you moved using your iPhone will be in the folder you moved it to. To move a message to a folder, bring up the message from your Inbox and tap the Move button on the bottom toolbar—its icon looks like an arrow pointing down over a folder. You will then be presented with a list of folders to move the message to. Tap the folder you want to move it to and your iPhone will move it. If you have a POP-based email account, you can still use this feature to move a message to the Drafts, Sent, or Trash folders. However, these folders only exist on your iPhone, so the message will not be moved to these folders on your computer.

Deleting an Email Message

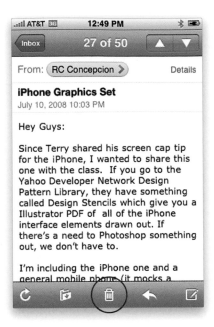

Once you've read a message and you decide that you don't need to keep it any longer, you can move the message to the Trash folder. While the message is displayed, you can tap the Trash button on the bottom toolbar to move the message to the Trash. For IMAP-based accounts, the message will be in the Trash or Deleted Items folder when you get back to your computer. Let's say you get a message that you know you want to delete without even reading it—you can do this right from the Inbox. Simply flick your finger across the message in the Inbox and a Delete button will appear. Tap the Delete button to delete the message. Lastly, you can also delete messages from the Inbox by tapping the Edit button at the top right of the Inbox and a circle will appear next to each message. You can tap the message you want to delete and the circle will turn red with a white checkmark. Once you've selected all the messages you want to delete, just tap the Delete button at the bottom of the screen to delete them.

Forwarding an Email

Sometimes you might want to forward a message that you've received to other contacts. To forward a message that you're viewing, tap the left-pointing arrow at the bottom of the screen. You will get a pop-up menu that offers a choice between Reply, (Reply All, if the message was sent to multiple people), Forward, and Cancel. Tap Forward and the message will come up with the cursor in the To field. You can then either key in the name of the contact that you want to forward it to, or the email address that you want to forward it to. If you start typing a name that is already one of your saved contacts, the iPhone will present you with a list of contacts to choose from. The more letters you type, the more it will narrow down the list. If you just want to choose a contact directly, you can tap the + (plus sign) button at the right side of the To field to choose one of your contacts. After putting in your first contact, if you want to forward this message to additional contacts, just start typing in a new name (or email address) and the list will pop up again for you to choose the contact that you want to forward this message to. You can also carbon copy (CC) or blind carbon copy (BCC) additional contacts.

Composing a New Email Message

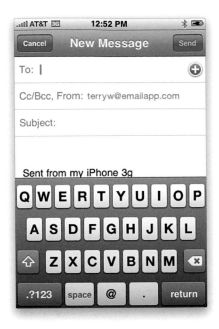

Being able to email on the go is one of the best features of the iPhone. To create a new email message from scratch, you must first go to the Mail application from the Home screen. Once you're there, you can tap the Compose button at the bottom right of the screen from your Mailboxes screen, Inbox (or other mailbox), or while you're viewing any email message. A blank email message will appear with the cursor in the To field. You can then either key in the name of the contact that you want to send it to, or the email address that you want to send it to. If you start typing a name that is already one of your saved contacts, the iPhone will present you with a list of contacts to choose from. The more letters you type, the more it will narrow down the list. If you just want to choose a contact directly, you can tap the + (plus sign) button at the right side of the To field to choose one of your contacts. After putting in your first contact, if you want to send this message to additional contacts, just start typing in a new name and the list will pop up again for you to choose the next contact that you want to send this message to. You can also carbon copy (CC) or blind carbon copy (BCC) additional contacts. Next, you'll want to key in a subject in the Subject field and then your message in the body field below. Your email can be as long as you like. Once you have your message addressed and composed, you can tap the Send button to send it. If you tap the Cancel button, you'll be given the opportunity to save it as a draft and continue it later.

Emailing a Photo

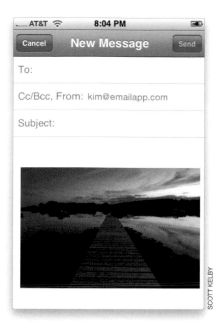

The iPhone has a built-in 2-megapixel camera and it supports syncing photos from your computer. You can email either the photos you take with the iPhone's camera or the ones that are already in your iPhone's Photo Library. To email a photo, go to the Home screen by pressing the Home button and then tap the Photos button. If you want to send a photo that you took with your iPhone's camera, then it will be in the Camera Roll folder. If you want to send a photo that you synced from your computer, then it will either be in the Photo Library or one of the albums that you brought over. Find the photo you want to send and tap on it. In the lower-left corner will be a rectangle with an arrow coming out of a box. Tap that button and you'll have the choice to Use As Wallpaper, Email Photo, or Assign to Contact. You want to tap the Email Photo option. This will put your photo into the body of a new message. You can then address the message to the contact or contacts that you want to send the photo to, give it a subject, and even key in some text in the body area above the Image. After you've got your message worded the way you want and addressed to your contact(s), just tap the Send button to send it off.

Emailing a Note

The iPhone has a Notes application and you can email any of the notes that you create. To email a note, tap the Notes button from the Home screen. If you have more than one note, you can navigate to the note you want to email by tapping the left or right arrows at the bottom of the Notes screen. Once you find the note you want to email, tap the Envelope button and this will copy your note into the body of a new email message. You can now address it to the contact(s) that you want to send it to. It also uses the note's title as the subject, which you can change if you want to. You can add or delete part of the note if you only want to send a portion of it or add to what was there. Once you have the email addressed, tap the Send button to send it on its way.

iTip

Not only can you email someone photos and notes, but you can also email someone a URL directly from Safari. While in Safari on the page that you want to send the URL for, tap the + (plus sign) button at the bottom. Tap the Mail Link to this Page button and it will generate a new email message with the URL of that page in the body. All you have to do is address the email to your contact(s) and tap Send.

Header Details

When you receive an email, you might want to see the details of who the message was actually addressed to. When you view a message, you'll see the word "Details" next to the From address. Tap Details to reveal all the names/email addresses of the people that the original message went to. Tap Hide to hide the details again.

iTip

If you tap one of the addresses in the Details area, including the sender, and they are not already one of your contacts, you will get the ability to create a new email to that person, as well as add them to your contacts.

Switching Between Accounts

If you have two or more email accounts set up on your iPhone, you can switch between them to view messages in each account's Inbox. Tap the Mail button on the Home screen and then if you're not already on the Accounts screen, you can get to it by tapping the Accounts button in the upper-left corner. Once you get to the Accounts screen, you can tap on any of your accounts to view email in that account.

Delete or Move Multiple Emails At Once

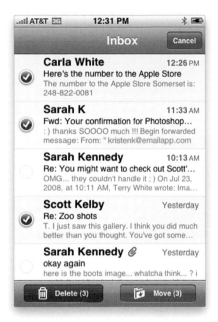

In iPhone's version 2 software, you can now delete or move multiple emails at once, which is a lot faster than having to delete or move them one by one. To delete multiple emails or move two or more emails to a folder, tap on the Mail button on the Home screen, then bring up your email list containing the emails you want to delete or move, and tap the Edit button in the upper-right corner. You will see a circle appear to the left of each message and if you tap each message you want to delete or move, this will put a checkmark in their circles. You can then either tap the Delete button at the bottom to move the selected messages to the Trash, or you can tap the Move button to get a list of folders and just tap on the folder you want the messages moved into.

Play Audio Attachments

I have the good fortune of having a voicemail system in my home office (PhoneValet) that can email received voicemails as audio attachments. When I receive these files on my iPhone, I can actually play them and hear them through the iPhone speaker or through my earbuds. If you receive a compatible audio attachment (like an MOV file), just tap on it in the body of the email, and it will play.

Chapter Four
Surfin' Safari
Using the iPhone's
Safari Web Browser

 Now you gotta admit—the Beach Boys' classic hit "Surfin' Safari" is just about as perfect a title for a chapter on using the Safari Web browser as you can get. But as you know, that's where the cohesiveness ends on this page, because the rest of this paragraph really has nothing to do with browsing the Web, or safaris, or even the iPhone for that matter. That's right, this is my "special time" where you and I get to bond on a level that I normally reserve only for close personal friends and men's room attendants. You see, when someone has read as much of this book as you have, a very magical thing happens. It's a magical moment of extreme clarity we both share simultaneously (but not at the same time), and although we experience this together, we do it totally separately, but still as one (which isn't easy to do). For example, it's that moment when you realize that you've already invested so much time in this book that you really can't stop now and you're "in it for the long haul." For me, it's the moment when I realize that you've had the book so long now you can't really return it for a refund. You see, it really is magical. So, put down the book, and take just a moment to close your eyes, breathe deeply, and just let your mind drift off to a place where it doesn't matter that the chapter introduction doesn't actually relate to the content in the coming chapter. That type of thing no longer matters to you because in your mind you're finally free—free to finally reach out and touch that existential neo-ocular nirvana that can only happen in Seattle. I have no idea how to end this gracefully. Hey! Quick—look over there!

Launching Safari

Safari is the iPhone's Web browser. It is by far the best Web browsing experience on a mobile phone to date. Safari will launch automatically when you tap on a URL (Web address) in one of the other applications. However, if you want to launch it manually, it's easy. Go to the Home screen and tap the Safari button at the bottom of the screen. The first time you launch Safari, it will launch to a blank screen.

Keying in a URL Manually

Once Safari is up and running, there will be an Address Bar at the top of the screen. You can tap in the Address Bar to bring up the keyboard. From there you can key in the URL of the website that you want to go to. There is even a .com button on the keyboard to help you complete your URL. Once you have the address keyed in, you can tap the Go button to go to it. If you want to type in another URL and there is one already there, you can clear it by tapping the X in a gray circle to the right of the address once you tap on the Address Bar.

 iTip

It's usually not necessary to key in the full address, such as http://www.creativesuitepodcast .com. Usually just keying in the domain name and the domain extension will work, such as creativesuitepodcast.com.

Navigating a Webpage

Once you get to the webpage that you keyed in the URL for, you should know the best ways to navigate within Safari. First, to scroll down the page you actually use your finger to flick the page up. Undoubtedly, in most cases the page will be too small to read. You can quickly zoom in on a page by double-tapping on the page. This will zoom the display nice and large. To move the page around, just use your finger to drag the page in the direction that you want to drag it in. To zoom out, double-tap the page again. You can also zoom in and out on a page using multi-touch. To zoom in on the page, use two fingers in a spreading out motion as if you're expanding the size of the page to zoom in. To zoom out on the page, use your two fingers to pinch the page as if you're making it smaller, because you are. As you navigate to different links, you can go back to a previous page by tapping the left-facing arrow at the bottom of the Safari screen. You can go forward by tapping the right-facing arrow.

---

iTip

Even when you're zoomed out on a page that is too small to read, the iPhone's Safari Web browser does an amazing job of letting you tap on links. I'm amazed at how accurate it is when I tap a button that I can barely read—it still knows where I'm trying to tap and takes me there. If you've scrolled down a long page, double-tapping on the time at the top of the screen will take you back up to the top of the webpage.

Using Your Bookmarks

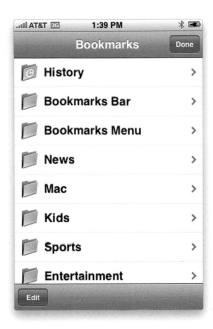

While keying in URLs can be fun, and good practice on the iPhone's keyboard, you'll probably want to take advantage of Bookmarks to get to your favorite sites. The iPhone automatically syncs your Bookmarks from Safari on your Mac or PC, or your Favorites in Internet Explorer on your PC (if you have this preference set). To use one of these Bookmarks on the iPhone, tap the little book button at the bottom of the Safari screen. All of your Bookmarks will be listed just as they appear on your computer. They'll be in the same folders and in the same order. Navigate to the Bookmark you want to use and tap it to go to that site.

---

iTip

Although the iPhone offers the best Web viewing experience on a mobile phone, you may find it slow loading some of the more graphic-intensive sites when you're not connected to Wi-Fi. Some of your favorite companies may offer a "mobile" or low-bandwidth version of their site so that you can get to the information you need without all the fluff. For example, check out iphone.fandango.com as opposed to www.fandango .com. You'll see that it gives you just what you need to see movie times and even buy tickets without loading all the pretty graphics.

Adding a Bookmark

Although the iPhone uses the same Bookmarks that are on your computer, you may discover a new site that you'd like to bookmark while you're out with your iPhone. If you have a page open in Safari that you'd like to bookmark, tap the + (plus sign) button at the bottom of the Safari screen and, from the options that appear, tap the Add Book-mark button. This will prompt you to name the Bookmark, which you can simply leave as the name of the page as it appears, or you could rename or shorten the name to your liking. You can also determine where it saves the Bookmark in your Bookmarks folder structure by tapping on the Bookmarks button below the URL. Once you're happy with the name and location of the Bookmark, tap the Save button to save the Bookmark.

iTip

I check movie times at my local AMC theater fairly often, and if you do the same, you'll love this website that looks, acts, and feels just like an iPhone application from Apple (even though it's actually a website). Just to go www.moviesapp.com, enter your zip code, choose your local theater, and you'll swear you're using an application (rather than a website). It has movie times, each movie's running time, you can watch the movie trailers, and you can even buy your tickets right there. You'll love it!

Editing a Bookmark

Sometimes website addresses change and you need to update your Bookmark. One great thing is that if you update a Bookmark on your computer, it will update in the iPhone the next time you sync (if you have this preference set) or over the air if you use MobileMe. However, if you want to update it right on the iPhone, you can. Launch Safari and tap the Bookmarks button at the bottom of the screen. This will bring up your Bookmarks list and you'll be able to navigate to the folder containing the Bookmark you want to edit. Next, tap the Edit button in the lower-left corner of the Bookmarks folder screen. Then tap the Bookmark you wish to edit. You'll be able to edit the name and the URL, as well as the Bookmark location. Once you've made your changes, tap the Bookmarks folder button in the upper-left corner of the screen to return to the list of Bookmarks. You can then tap the Done button when you're done making edits.

Deleting a Bookmark

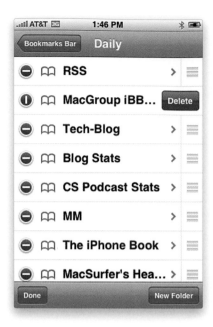

If you have a site bookmarked that you no longer need, you can delete it right from your iPhone. With the Safari application open, tap the Bookmarks button to bring up your list of Bookmarks. Navigate to the folder screen that lists the Bookmark that you wish to delete. Tap the Edit button in the lower-left corner and each Bookmark will have a – (minus sign) in a red circle to the left of it. Tap the red circle next to the Bookmark you want to delete, and then a Delete button will appear for that Bookmark. Tap the Delete button and that Bookmark will be deleted forever.

Adding a Web Clip

If there are websites that you go to very often, you can now add them directly to your Home screen, and you can even have it scroll to the area of the page that you always check out. Just tap the Safari button on the Home screen, then go to the website you want to add (feel free to zoom in on it if you like), and tap the + (plus sign) button at the bottom of the Safari screen. From the options that appear, tap on Add to Home Screen, and you'll then see the screen shown above, which allows you to name your Home screen button. So, just name your new button (or leave the one already there for you) and tap the Add button at the top right. A new button for this website will now appear on your Home screen. If the website is iPhone-aware, then you'll have a nice little icon representing the logo of the site. If not, it will show you a miniaturized representation of the page.

Multiple Home Screens

Now that you can add your own Web clips and other applications (for adding new applications, see Chapter 6) to the Home screen, the iPhone lets you have up to nine Home screens. When you have two or more Home screens, you will see two or more little dots above the Dock at the bottom of the Home screen, indicating how many Home screens you have and which screen you're looking at (its dot appears white). You can either tap one of the dots to switch screens or you can flick the screens left or right like you would navigate your pictures.

Rearrange Your Home Screen Icons

When you add your own Web clips and other applications to the Home screen, you may find that you want to rearrange them and you can even rearrange the ones that came with the iPhone. To rearrange the buttons on the Home screen, tap-and-hold on one of the icons for just a few seconds and all your Home screen icons will start wiggling. You can now touch-and-drag them around in to the order you want. Once you're satisfied with your new arrangement, just press the Home button to lock them in place.

---

iTip

If there are applications or Web clips that you don't use often, you can move those items to another Home screen, since the iPhone allows you to have up to nine Home screens. Just tap-and-hold on an icon until they start to wiggle. Then touch-and-drag your less-frequently used icons to the right side of the screen. The iPhone will automatically advance to the next Home screen and take your icon with it. Once you're done, tap the Home button to lock in your changes.

Removing a Web Clip

If you decide you no longer want one of your custom Web clips (or an application that you installed—see Chapter 6 for more on applications) on your Home screen, you can remove it. Tap-and-hold for a few seconds on the Web clip icon that you want to remove, until the icons start to wiggle. You'll then see a little X in the upper-left corner of each Web clip (and application that can be removed). To delete the Web clip you no longer want on your Home screen, simply tap the little X and then tap Delete from the dialog that appears. It will disappear, and your remaining icons will reshuffle. Once you're done, tap the Home button to stop the icons from wiggling and lock them in place.

Using Google or Yahoo Search

It's great to be able to go to sites that you already know by either keying in the URL or using your Bookmarks. However, it's even more fun sometimes discovering new sites. You can search for sites right on your iPhone using two of the industry's leading search engines. The iPhone is set to Google's search engine by default. However, if you prefer Yahoo, you can make Yahoo the default by changing your preference in the Safari settings (tap on the Settings button on the Home screen). To use your default search engine, launch Safari from the Home screen. Then tap the Address Bar to bring it up along with the keyboard. Now tap on the search field and type in your search terms. Once you've typed in your search terms, tap the Google (or Yahoo) button on the bottom right of the keyboard to begin your search. Once your search results come up, you can then tap on any of the links to go to any of the pages that you want to visit.

---

iTip

If you want to send a website link to someone, just tap on the + (plus sign) button at the bottom of the Safari screen, then tap Mail Link to this Page, and it will create a new email with the URL that was in the Address Bar in the body of the email message. This way you can send someone a Web address with a single tap.

Viewing Your Pages Horizontally

The iPhone has an amazing feature that automatically detects when it is rotated 90° in either direction. This works great in Safari to allow you to view your pages in a horizontal view. Depending on the layout of the page, this could mean not having to scroll or zoom in as much. To use this feature, simply navigate to the page you want to view horizontally in Safari. Then hold your iPhone up (the sensor doesn't work so well when the iPhone is lying down) and rotate it 90°. The display will automatically refresh with the new orientation. You can use all the same options while in this mode, including the keyboard.

iTip
If you press-and-hold your finger down on a text link or graphic link on a webpage, a little pop-up window will appear showing the URL that the link will take you to.

Dialing a Phone Number on a Webpage

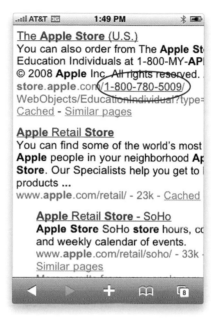

Oftentimes we search for companies on the Web not only to research them, but also to call them. If you search for a company in Safari or navigate to any page that has a phone number on it, chances are the iPhone will recognize that phone number as a phone number and it will be highlighted. You can tap the phone number and the iPhone will ask you to confirm whether or not you want to dial it. If you tap Call, you'll be taken to the Phone application automatically, where your call will be placed. Once you tap End Call, you'll be returned to Safari to the page you were last viewing.

Navigating Back and Forth

Safari on the iPhone supports two ways of browsing: The first way is the traditional browsing method that as you tap on links on a page, the page you are currently viewing is replaced by the new page. This is how every browser that you've ever used works. The other way is a cross between spawning new pages and the tabbed browsing you're used to in Safari or Internet Explorer on your computer. By default, when you tap a link on a page in Safari on your iPhone, Safari goes to that page by replacing the page you were currently looking at. To go back to the previous page, tap the left arrow at the bottom of the Safari screen. Once you go back at least one page, you can go forward by tapping the right arrow.

---

iTip

If you're on a webpage that is long and requires scrolling, you can of course flick your finger to scroll the page, or you can double-tap to zoom in on the page and then double-tap in the lower half of the page to scroll down a screen at a time (just be sure to tap in a blank area of the page).

Getting a New Page

Sometimes you may want to keep viewing the page in Safari that you're looking at and have the flexibility of going to a different page without losing the current page. To do this, tap the little Pages button in the lower-right corner of the Safari screen. This will shrink your current page down and a New Page button will appear in the lower-left corner. Tap the New Page button to create a blank page in Safari. Now you can either key in a new URL, do a search, or use your Bookmarks to go to the page you want to go to.

Navigate Between Pages in Safari

Once you have two or more pages open in Safari, you can navigate back and forth between them. To go to another open page in Safari, tap the Pages button in the lower-right corner of the Safari screen. Then, by flicking your finger across the page towards the left or the right, you can navigate between your open pages. Once you get to the page you want to view, just tap it to bring it back up to full screen. This is really handy when you're trying to compare things such as prices or schedules between two different sites at once.

📶 **iTip**

Want to add a great game of blackjack to your iPhone (it's not really an application—it's a website that looks and acts just like an iPhone application, but it's actually just a website)? Then go to http://mynumo.com/iphone/bj/blackjack.htm.

Refreshing a Page

Safari does a good job of keeping the page you're currently viewing in place when you switch between applications. However, if you're finding that you want to know the latest bid on that eBay item you're watching, you may need to refresh the page. You can refresh just about any page in the Safari browser on the iPhone by tapping the circular arrow button in the upper-right corner of the Safari window to the right of the Address Bar. This will cause Safari to go out to the Web server for the page you're viewing and grab the latest version of it.

Viewing RSS Feeds on the iPhone

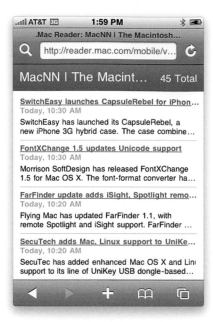

The Safari browser on the iPhone does support RSS (Really Simple Syndication) feeds. Most news sites, blogs, and corporate sites today provide RSS feeds so that users can subscribe to them and check the feed rather than constantly going directly to the site to see if it's been updated. Some sites actually have the links to their various RSS feeds right on their homepages. However, it's easier to bookmark and organize these feeds on your computer rather than doing it on the iPhone. On your computer, use Safari (available for both Mac and PC) and go to some of your favorite sites. You will see an RSS button at the right side of the Address Bar if the site has a feed. Click the RSS button to take you to the feed page for that particular site. This is the page you'll want to bookmark. I place all my RSS feeds in a folder called (wait for it) RSS on my Bookmarks Bar. When you're done setting up your RSS folder, sync your computer and your iPhone to update your Bookmarks. Now when you're on the iPhone, you can tap any feed in that folder to see all the current headlines for that site.

---

iTip

You might also want to check out Google's Web-based RSS reader. This reader works nicely on the iPhone and you can find the RSS feed on Google's News page.

Filling in an Online Form on Your iPhone

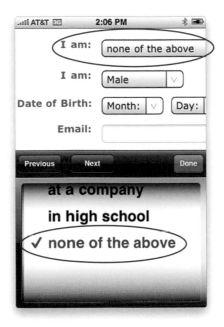

At some point you're going to go to a website in Safari on your iPhone that requests some type of information. You could be placing an online order at your favorite etailer or simply keying in your username and password on your favorite community site. When you get to a form on a webpage, you can tap on the first field on that page, which will zoom in on the field and bring up the keyboard. You can type out your response for the first field, and then if the second field is still in view, you can just tap it and keep typing. If the next field is not in view, you can tap Done on the keyboard, which will zoom the page back out again and then you can tap the field you want to go to next and the keyboard will reappear. If you tap on a pop-up menu on a page, Safari does something very cool: it magnifies the list of choices and puts them in a flick wheel that you can spin with your finger to get to the right option. Once you've got your form all filled out, you can dismiss the keyboard by tapping Done and then tap the submit button for your form to submit your data.

Closing a Page

Having multiple-page support in Safari is awesome. However, when you're finished viewing a page, there is no reason to have it out there hanging around. To close a page in Safari that you no longer need open, tap the Pages button in the lower-right corner of the Safari screen. Navigate to the page you wish to close and tap the little red X in the upper-left corner of the page. The page will close and you'll be switched to a page that is still open.

MMS Support—Kind Of

The iPhone still doesn't support MMS (multimedia messaging), so there is no way to send a photo, for example, directly to another cell phone without using email. Although Apple may add this feature in a future update, there is currently no way to send an MMS message on the iPhone. However, if you receive an MMS message, AT&T has stepped in with a solution (check with your carrier if you don't have AT&T). AT&T has a website set up at www.viewmymessage.com. When you receive an MMS message on your iPhone, you'll get a text message stating that you have received a multimedia message, and it will also give you the viewmymessage.com site with a special login and password just for that message. You can then tap the viewmymessage.com link in the text message and view the message directly in Safari on the iPhone. *Note:* See page 259 in Chapter 9 for a workaround tip on how to send an MMS message.

Chapter Five

Tool Time

iPhone's Tools for Organizing Your Life

 Are we now to the point that our lives have become so complex, so chaotic, and so congealed (congealed?) that the only way to keep track of it all is to buy a hand-held device which becomes the center around which our lives revolve as it shouts out alarms, and commands us to be in certain places at certain times? All this while we're trying to monitor the markets, and stay in contact with people on different continents, in different time zones, and the only way we feel we can find the location of the nearest coffee shop is to send a request to a satellite in geosynchronous orbit above the earth requesting that it not only point out the location of said coffee shop, but that it ping a different satellite to provide a detailed photographic image of its roof? Is this what we've come to? Yes, yes it is, but I'm totally okay with it. Why? Because I bought stock in numerous GPS satellite companies, Google, and Starbucks. Okay, I really didn't buy stock in those companies but I could have, and I could have done it right from my iPhone. Well, at least until my wife found out, because at that moment you would've heard that cast-iron sound of a frying pan connecting with a husband's head (the one you hear in cartoons), but it would've been so loud that they would've heard it aboard the International Space Station (which is in geosynchronous orbit high above the earth, by the way), and when the astronauts heard it, they'd look at each other, nod, and say, "I bet some guy's wife just found out he bought a whole bunch of stock using his iPhone." You know, it really is a small world after all.

Setting Up Clocks for Different Time Zones

If you do business internationally, or in different times zones, then you can set up world clocks to show the time in each city. Start at the Home screen and tap on Clock. Then tap on World Clock at the bottom-left corner of the screen to bring up the World Clock screen. By default, it shows the current time in Cupertino, California. To delete Cupertino as one of your cities, tap the Edit button in the upper-left corner, and a red circle with a – (minus sign) appears before the word "Cupertino." Tap that red circle once and a Delete button appears on the right. Tap Delete and it's gone (the clock—not Cupertino itself). To add a new city, tap the + (plus sign) button in the top-right corner to bring up a city search field and keyboard. Type in the city you want to add (in our example here, I typed in Detroit, USA. Actually, I just typed in "det" and Detroit, USA appeared in the list). When your city appears in the list, just tap on it and it's added as a clock. To add more cities, just tap the + button again.

---

iTip

Why does the default time in the World Clock screen show Cupertino, California? It's because that's where Apple's headquarters (also known as "the mothership" to Macintosh fanatics) is located.

Using the Stopwatch

I love this stopwatch feature because it's just so simple, efficient, and it has a really large readout. To get to it, start at the Home screen and tap on Clock. Then tap on Stopwatch at the bottom of the screen to bring up the Stopwatch screen. There are only two buttons: Start and Reset. To start timing something, tap the green Start button. Once the stopwatch starts running, the green Start button is replaced by a red Stop button. To start over, tap the Reset button. If you want to record lap times, just tap the Lap button (what used to be the Reset button before the stopwatch started running), and those times are listed in the fields below the two buttons. You can have lots of individual lap times (I stopped at 32 laps—man, was I tired), and you can scroll through the list of lap times just like you would scroll any list—by swiping your finger on the screen in the direction you want to scroll.

---

iTip

When you're looking at the time in the World Clock screen, if the clock's face is white, that means it's daytime in that city. If the clock's face is black, it's night.

Setting Up a Countdown Clock

If you need to count down a particular length of time (let's say you're baking and you need to know when it's been 45 minutes), then you can set a countdown timer to alert you after 45 minutes has passed. To do this, start at the Home screen and tap on Clock. Then tap on Timer at the bottom-right corner of the screen to bring up the Timer screen. You can scroll the Hours and Minutes wheels onscreen to set the amount of time you want to count down to. Just below the countdown wheels is a button called When Timer Ends, and this is where you choose either the ringtone that your iPhone will play when the countdown clock hits zero, or you can choose to have the iPhone simply go to sleep (which is great if you want to play music for a specific amount of time before you fall asleep, and then have the iPhone put itself to sleep to save battery life while you're sleeping). Once you've set your countdown time, and selected what happens when the timer hits zero (by tapping the When Timer Ends button), just tap the green Start button and the countdown begins.

Using Your iPhone as an Alarm

You don't have to take that travel alarm clock with you on the road anymore, because your iPhone has a great alarm clock built right in. Start at the Home screen and tap on Clock. Then tap on Alarm at the bottom of the screen to bring up the Alarm screen. To add an alarm, tap on the + (plus sign) button up in the top-right corner of the screen. This brings up the Add Alarm screen, where you can choose a variety of options, including whether, and how often, to repeat this alarm, what sound will play when the alarm goes off, whether to allow you to snooze the alarm, and the name of the custom alarm you just created (that way, you can save custom alarms, which is handy if you have to wake up at different times on different days. You can have one alarm for home, one for travel on weekdays, one for travel on weekends, etc.). When you've configured your alarm the way you want it, tap Save and your alarm appears in your Alarm list, and it's turned on. At the designated time, your alarm sounds (and will keep sounding) until you tap on one of two buttons that now appear onscreen: (1) Snooze (if you turned that feature on), or (2) OK. If you tap Snooze, the alarm sound stops, but it will re-sound in 10 minutes. If you tap OK, it turns the alarm off. Also, if you want to activate an alarm you've already created, you can turn on/off alarms in the Alarm list. To turn on a particular alarm, tap the gray button. To turn it back off, tap the gray button again.

Using the Calculator

Having a calculator on the iPhone is handy and in the iPhone's Version 2 software, the Calculator feature got much better. When you tap on Calculator on your Home screen, it will bring up a basic calculator. This calculator does all the basic functions that you would expect, such as add, subtract, multiply, and divide, and it has a built-in memory function, too. If you want a more sophisticated scientific calculator (with sine, cosine, tangent, logarithm, etc.), just rotate your iPhone 90° and you'll get the Scientific Calculator instead of the basic one. Pretty neat!

---

iTip

If you make a mistake while entering a series of numbers, you don't have to start over again. Just tap the C key once and that will perform a Clear Entry, and then you can simply re-enter the number.

Finding Videos on YouTube

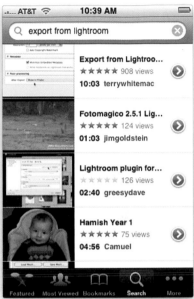

You can watch videos from the wildly popular online video sharing site YouTube.com right from your iPhone. It doesn't actually download the videos from YouTube.com onto your iPhone—you search for videos you want to watch, and then you watch them on your iPhone just like you would watch YouTube.com videos on your computer. However, you can bookmark your favorite videos and get right to them. Start at the Home screen and tap on YouTube. Then tap on Search (at the bottom of the screen) to bring up a search field. Tap on the search field to bring up the keyboard, type in your search term(s), then tap the Search button to search YouTube's vast video library. The results appear in a list below the search field. To watch one of these videos, just tap on it, then turn your iPhone sideways (videos always play in this wide mode). To see more about a video in the list, tap the blue arrow button to the right of the video in the results list.

 iTip

When you're using the Weather application, and you see little dots below the Weather screen, that's telling you that there are more screens (in other words, you're monitoring other cities). To see them, you just need to swipe across the screen with your finger. For example, if you see three dots, there are two other screens. This also holds true for webpages—if you see four dots, you've got four webpages open (to see them, just swipe).

Playing YouTube Videos on Your iPhone

When a video first starts playing, a set of video controls appears onscreen for pausing the video, adjusting the volume, etc. There's even a button to email a YouTube video link to a friend. To bring back those controls, just touch the screen. To return to the search results list, tap the blue Done button in the top-left corner, then on the info screen for the video, tap the Search button in the top left.

iTip

There are little left and right arrow buttons that appear at the bottom of any note in the Notes app, and tapping on either one takes you to either the previous note (the left arrow), or the next note in the list (the right arrow).

Saving YouTube Videos as Favorites

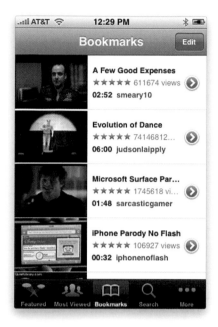

To bookmark a video you like (so you can jump directly to it next time), tap on the Bookmarks button in the video controls (at the bottom of the screen while it's playing) or the Bookmark button beneath the video's info (to the left of the Share button when you're done playing the video). Also, at the bottom of the YouTube screen are buttons that take you directly to the Featured videos of the day, YouTube's Most Viewed videos, and videos that you've bookmarked. If you tap the More button, you'll see a new set of menus which let you jump to YouTube's Most Recent videos, see their Top Rated videos, or see a History (list) of the YouTube videos you've already watched.

Customizing the YouTube Buttons

Although a default set of buttons appears in a bar at the bottom of the main YouTube screen, you can customize this bar to contain the YouTube buttons you use the most. To do this, start at the Home screen and tap YouTube, then tap the More button. When the More screen appears (and you see the row of buttons across the bottom), tap the Edit button in the top-right corner of the screen to bring up the Configure screen. Now you just press-and-hold your finger on any button you'd like to appear on your bar, and simply drag it down to the bar and hold it over the button you want to replace. The button to be replaced gets a large white glow around it, and once you see that, you simply take your finger off the screen and your new button appears in that spot. That's all there is to it.

Using Maps to Find Just About Anything

The iPhone's built-in Maps feature is pretty darn amazing—it lets you instantly find anything from the nearest golf course to a dry cleaner in the next city you're traveling to, and can not only give you precise directions on how to get there, it can call your destination, as well. Here's how to use it: Start at the Home screen and tap on Maps. When the Maps screen appears, you'll see a search field at the top where you can enter an address you'd like to see on the map. However, before you type in your search, tap the circular Locate Me button in the lower-left corner, so that the iPhone will know where you are. Then it will find the location of the business that you search for that is closest to you. For example, let's say you'd like to find the nearest Krispy Kreme donut shop (not that I would actually ever search for one. Wink, wink). You'd tap once on the search field to bring up the keyboard, then you'd type in the name of the business, and tap the Search button. In the example shown above, I entered "Krispy Kreme," and on the Google map of my area, red pushpins appeared on the two nearest locations. A little pop-up appears with the name of the location that is closest, and if you tap the blue arrow button in that pop-up, it takes you to an Info screen for that particular location. If you tap the phone number, it dials it for you (that way you could call and ask, "Is the Hot Now sign on?" Ya know, if you were so inclined). If you want to find a business that isn't near you, just add the city into the search. For example, typing "Krispy Kreme, Atlanta, Georgia" would locate the ones in, or close to, Atlanta, Georgia.

Locate Yourself on the Map

The iPhone uses cell towers, as well as Wi-Fi hotspots, to triangulate your location. If you have an iPhone 3G, it can use cell towers, Wi-Fi hotspots, and a built-in GPS to find where you are on the map. Tap the Maps button on the Home screen, then tap the Locate Me button at the bottom left of the screen to have the iPhone locate your position on the map. Once the iPhone knows where you are, Maps can then be used to search the surrounding area for the nearest businesses and services that you want to find. Just type "pizza" in the search field, tap Search, and Maps will locate all the local pizza joints close to your location.

Getting Driving Directions

You can use the iPhone's Maps feature to get step-by-step driving directions to any location, and from any location. Here's how: Start at the Home screen and tap on Maps. Let's say you want directions to your favorite restaurant—for me, it's Maggiano's Little Italy. Tap the Search button at the bottom of the Maps screen, then type in the name of the location you want to drive to—in my case, Maggiano's—and tap the Search button. Once it drops a pin on the map for the restaurant you want to drive to (if there is more than one pin, tap on the pin for the location you want), tap the little blue arrow button to the right of the pin's name. This will bring up the Info screen for the restaurant, including the phone number, so you can call and make reservations. Now tap the Directions To Here button on the Info screen, and this will take you to the Directions screen. Just tap the Route button, and the iPhone automatically figures out where you are and plots your route accordingly. If you want turn-by-turn directions, just tap the little curled page button at the bottom right of the Overview screen showing your route, and tap List. This will give you turn-by-turn directions. If you have an iPhone 3G, which has built-in GPS, the iPhone can even track you along on your route as you drive.

Drop a Pin on the Map

There will be times that you may not know the name of the business, or even the address, you're trying to get to. No problem! If you can find its general location on the map, you can use the Drop Pin feature to put a pin anywhere on the map you'd like. Once that pin is in place, you can then use it as a reference point to get directions from where you are to the location that is marked by the pin. Tap on Maps from the Home screen. Next, navigate the map to the general vicinity that you want to go to—you can do a search for a city, or a street, or anything else that's in the area. Then, click the little curled page button in the lower-right corner of the screen to expose the additional Maps options. Tap on Drop Pin to put a pin on the map. You can then move the pin around by just tapping on it and dragging it with your finger. Once the pin is in place, tap the pin, then tap the blue arrow button, and tap Directions To Here. This brings up the Directions screen, where you can tap the Next button at the bottom, and the iPhone will plot a route from your current location to the location of the pin.

Display More Information on the Map

The iPhone not only has the ability to show your location and route, but it also can show a satellite view and even the current traffic conditions. To get to these options, just tap the curled page button in the lower-right corner of any of the Maps screens. Tapping Map shows you an illustrated map of the location that you search; Satellite will show you an actual satellite photo of the location you search; and Hybrid shows you the Satellite view with the street names—this is kind of the best of both worlds. Tapping List will show you turn-by-turn driving directions. The Show Traffic button adds real-time traffic flow info for the major highways (green for more than 50 mph, yellow for 25–50 mph, red for less than 25 mph, and gray if there's no data).

Finding Your Contacts on the Map

If you've included a street address for your contact, you're just a couple of taps away from seeing their house on the map. Just go to the All Contacts list, tap on their name or do a search to find them, and when their Info screen appears, tap once on their address. This automatically takes you to the Maps app and pinpoints their address on the map. Better yet, once the map appears, tap on the curled page button in the lower-right corner of the screen, then tap on the Satellite button, and it shows you a satellite photo of their house. To zoom in for a closer look, just double-tap on their location on the screen. Each double-tap will zoom you in that much closer.

iTip

In the Maps application, if you're having the map give you directions from one loca-tion to another, it's usually helpful to tap the curled page button, then tap the List button (near the bottom-right corner of the screen), so you see a street-by-street, turn-by-turn list of the directions. But that's not the tip. The tip is: if you tap on any of those directions, it instantly switches back to Map view to pinpoint exactly where that list item appears on the map between the two locations.

Use Map Bookmarks

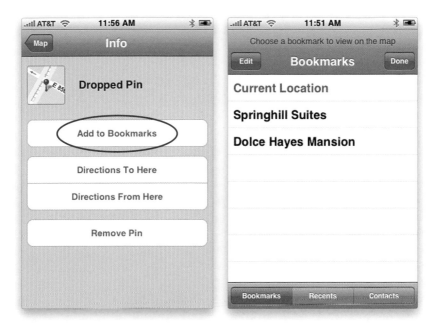

If you're traveling and you want to always be able to get back to the same place or have the same starting point (say your hotel) for each location you want to get a route to (or you get directions to places from home or work a lot), you can save your favorite locations as Book-marks. You can create a Maps Bookmark from any of your search results or a dropped pin. Just tap the blue arrow button to the right of the pin's name that you wish to create a Bookmark for, and then tap Add to Bookmarks. You'll be given the opportunity to name the Bookmark whatever you like. Then tap the Save button. Now, the next time you want directions to or from that location, you can use your Bookmark as a start or end destination in the Directions fields. Just tap Directions and then tap in either the Start or End field and you'll see a little Bookmarks button on the right (if the field already has a location in it, simply tap the little X at the right end of the field to clear it). Tap the Bookmarks button to bring up your list of Bookmarks to choose from. Then you can use any of your Bookmarks as a start or end point of reference. Tap the Route button, and you'll be on your way.

 iTip

The iPhone will also keep track of your most recent Maps searches, so even if you didn't bookmark a location that you recently searched for, it may still be in your Recents (tap the Recents button at the bottom of the Bookmarks screen) and therefore accessible as a start or end point.

Seeing Your Local Weather

You can set up your iPhone so you're only one tap away from seeing your current local weather, and a six-day forecast, as well. Start at the Home screen and tap on Weather. This brings up the weather forecast for Cupertino, California. You can change it to give your local weather by tapping once on the little "i" button in the bottom right of the screen. This brings up the Weather screen, where you'll see Cupertino listed with a little red circular button with a – (minus sign) in it. Tap on that button and a Delete button will appear to the right. Tap it and the weather for Cupertino is deleted. (By the way, there are two buttons at the bottom of this screen, so you can choose to display your weather in Fahrenheit or Celsius.) To add your own city's weather, tap on the + (plus sign) in the top-left corner and, using the keyboard at the bottom of the screen, type in your city and state or city and country (in the example shown here, I typed in "48034"), then tap the Search button. It will then display your city in a list (provided, of course, that it found your city), and all you have to do now is tap on your city name, then tap the blue Done key in the upper-right corner, and you're just a tap away from your local weather.

---

iTip

If you have multiple cities set up in Weather, instead of swiping the screen with your finger to change to the next city, you can tap the dots that appear under the weather display to go back and forth through your city locations.

Adding Weather for Other Cities

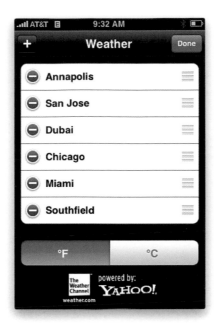

To add the weather for additional cities, you start out pretty much the same way as shown on the previous page —tap on that little "i" Icon at the bottom of your local weather screen, and when the next screen appears, tap the + (plus sign) in the top-left corner of the screen to add a new city. Type in the city and state (or city and country), then tap the Search button. When it finds your city, tap on it, then tap the Done button. At this point, you can also reorder the cities by tapping on the triple-line icon to the right of each city and dragging them up or down in the list. Although your new city is added, you won't see it when you first tap the Weather button. You have to slide your finger on the screen (just like you do with photos in the Photos application) to see other cities you're monitoring. So basically, you slide your local weather out of the way, and the next city slides into place. To return to your local city, slide back in the opposite direction. By the way, on the bottom-left corner of each weather forecast screen is a little Yahoo! logo. Tap on that logo, and it takes you to a Yahoo! webpage with information about that city, including a city guide, today's calendar of events, photos, and more.

 iTip

The color of the Weather screen lets you know whether it's day or night in the city you're looking at. If the Weather screen appears in blue, it's daytime, and if it's a dark purple, it's night.

Making Quick Notes

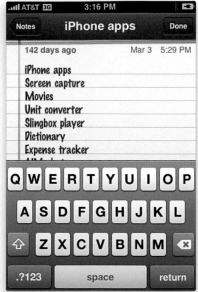

There's a Notes application for taking quick notes you want stored on your iPhone. To get there, start at the Home screen, then tap the Notes button. When the Notes screen appears, you'll see a list of any notes you've already taken. If you haven't created any notes yet, it figures you're there to create a new note, so it takes you to (no big surprise) the New Note screen. Type in your note (using the keyboard at the bottom of the screen), then tap the Done button in the upper-right corner when you're finished. This hides the keyboard and displays your note full screen. To return to your list of notes, tap the Notes button in the top-left corner. To read any note in the list, just tap on it (each note automatically displays the date and time it was created at the top of the note). To delete a note, tap on it, then in the next screen tap on the Trash button at the bottom of the screen.

---

iTip

In the Notes application, to quickly edit an existing note, just tap on it in the Notes list. Then when the note appears full screen, just tap anywhere on the note, and the keyboard appears—ready for editing. When you tap, if you tap on a word, your cursor appears right on that word. If you want to add to a note, tap just below your text.

Getting Stock Quotes

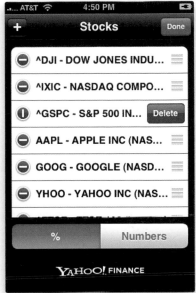

You can monitor the current quotes for stocks in your portfolio directly from your iPhone. Start at the Home screen, then tap the Stocks button. When the Stocks screen appears, by default, it shows the Dow Jones Industrial Average and a few other stock indexes, along with a default list of stocks (Apple, Google, Yahoo, and AT&T). You can delete any of these and add your own stocks to monitor by first tapping on the little "i" icon in the bottom-right corner of the screen. This brings up a list of the current indexes and stocks being monitored with a red circular – (minus sign) button before each listing. Tap on the red – button for the stock you want to remove and a Delete button appears to its right. Tap the Delete button and that stock is removed. To add a new stock (or index), tap the + (plus sign) button in the upper-left corner, which brings up the Add Stock screen. Type in the company name, index name, or stock symbol (if you know it) on the keyboard, then tap the blue Search button at the bottom-right corner of the screen. When it finds your company, it will display it in a list. Tap on the company name and it's added to your list of stocks. To add more stocks, tap the + button again. When you're done, tap the blue Done key in the upper-right corner. You can add as many stocks as you'd like, and to see other listings, just scroll down the screen by swiping (Apple calls it "flicking") your finger from the bottom of the screen up.

Getting More Info on Your Stocks

To see a chart of your stock's performance over time, just tap on the stock and a graph will appear at the bottom of the screen. To change the time frame of the chart, just tap on the list of time frames at the top of the chart (they range from 1 day to 2 years). For even more information on your currently selected stock, tap on the little Yahoo! logo that appears in the bottom-left corner of the Stocks screen, and it takes you to a Yahoo Finance webpage with detailed information about the company, including recent news articles. To return to your Stocks screen, press the Home button, then tap on Stocks.

---

iTip

To toggle between displaying the stock price's gain or loss in number and the gain/loss as a percentage, just tap directly on the numbers themselves (if the stock is showing a gain, the numbers appear with a green background. If the stock is showing a loss, the background is red).

Using Stocks as a Currency Converter

The Stocks application has a hidden feature—you can also use it as a currency converter, and have current conversion rates at all times. You will need to know the official three-character symbol for the currency you want to track. Tap on the Stocks app on the Home screen and then tap the little "i" icon in the lower-right corner. Now tap the + (plus sign) button in the upper-left corner as if you were adding a new stock. Type in the first currency code, followed by the second currency code, and then "=X" with no spaces. For example, if I wanted the conversion from U.S. dollars to euros, I would key in USDEUR=X and, as you can see in the example on the left above, it brought up the proper conversion in the search results. Now tap the result you want and then tap Done. The main Stocks screen will then show you up-to-date currency conversions whenever you go to it. In my example on the right above, I'm tracking the U.S. dollar against the Canadian dollar, the euro, and the South African rand.

Syncing Your Calendar

The iPhone has a built-in Calendar application, and depending on which calendar program you're using on your computer, you can sync your calendar directly into your iPhone (or you can manually add info to your calendar directly from your iPhone, as you'll learn on the next page). You can sync calendar info from either Apple's iCal or Microsoft Entourage on a Macintosh (see Chapter 10 for how to set up Entourage), or if you use Windows, you can sync your calendar from Microsoft Outlook. You can configure iTunes to sync with one of these apps and it will sync your calendar information with your iPhone automatically (if you have that preference set). If you're a corporate user with a Microsoft Exchange account or a MobileMe user, you can sync your calendar over the air, as well. To see your synced calendar info, start at the Home screen and tap the Calendar button. You can view your calendar as one long scrolling list or in a more traditional calendar view. To view by day, tap the Day button at the bottom of the screen, or tap Month to view the entire month (as shown here). In the Month view, if you see a small dot appearing below the date, that means you have an event scheduled for some-time that day. To see the event, tap once directly on that day and that day's events will appear below the calendar. If you tap the Day view, it shows you the entire day by time, starting at 12:00 a.m. In Day view, you can navigate to other nearby dates by tapping the left or right arrow buttons near the top of the screen. Any time you want to jump to today's events, just tap the Today button in the bottom-left corner of the screen.

Adding Appointments to Your Calendar

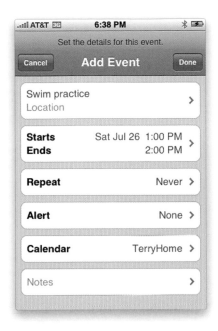

To add an appointment (event) to your iPhone's calendar, you could of course just add it on your computer and then sync your iPhone and your computer, but if you need to manually enter an appointment, it's easy. Start at the Home screen, then tap Calendar. In the Calendar screen, press the + (plus sign) button in the upper-right corner of the screen to bring up the Add Event screen. To give your event a name, tap on the Title field and the keyboard appears so you can type in a title (and a location, if you like). Tap Save, then tap on the Starts/Ends field to set the time when your event starts and ends. This brings up the Start & End screen. It chooses Starts by default, and you can choose the start time for your event by using the scroll wheels at the bottom of the screen. Then tap on Ends and choose the ending time. If this event runs the entire day, turn on the All-Day button by tapping on it. When you're done, tap the blue Save button. When you return to the Add Event screen, there are also options for repeating this appointment (for example, let's say you have a company meeting every Monday at 9:00 a.m.—you can tap Repeat, and when the Repeat Event screen appears, you can choose Every Week, and it will add that event to your calendar every Monday at 9:00 a.m. automatically). If you'd like your iPhone to give you a reminder alarm before your event, tap the Alert button. In the Event Alert screen that appears, tap how long before the event you want the alarm to go off, then tap the Save button at the top of the screen. If you have multiple calendars, you can also choose which calendar you want this appointment added to. When everything's just the way you want it, tap the blue Done button in the top-right corner.

Secure Your iPhone with a Passcode

No one plans to lose their iPhone or have it stolen. So if you want a little peace of mind, secure your iPhone with a passcode lock. This will prevent the person that finds it from accessing any of your data. To set a passcode, tap on Settings on the Home screen and then tap on General. Tap on Passcode Lock to turn it on. In the Set Passcode screen, you will be prompted to enter a four-digit passcode. On the Passcode Lock screen that appears, you'll also be able to set an interval for when the iPhone automatically locks by tapping the Require Passcode button. The intervals are Immediately, After 1 Minute, After 5 Minutes, After 15 Minutes, After 1 Hour, and After 4 Hours. The shorter the time, the more secure the phone will be. *Note:* Don't worry about having to fumble to enter the code when the phone rings. You only have to enter your passcode when you're making calls or before you go to do other functions. There is also no need to enter the passcode to make an emergency (911) call or to control your iPod application.

Chapter Six

The Song Remains the Same

Using iTunes, the iTunes Store, and the App Store

 Any chapter that is named after a Led Zeppelin movie from 1976 has to get some special credit in rock 'n' roll heaven, right? This is another movie I never saw, but I'm pretty sure it had Jimmy Stewart and Ann Margaret in it at some point. Didn't it? Anyway, this chapter is about how to use iTunes and the iTunes Store (which used to be called the iTunes Music Store until Apple added TV shows, movies, and the new App Store, and then it seemed silly to still call it a music store, especially when it had huge hit movies in it like *Star Trek: The Wrath of Khan* [that was with Leonardo DiCaprio and Ellen DeGeneres, wasn't it?] and *Zoolander* [with Meryl Streep and David Niven, I believe]). Anyway, here's the thing: in this chapter I will endeavor to help those who (a) have never had an iPod, and thus (b) never used iTunes, which means you've (c) never been to the iTunes Store, which means (d) you're not a teen, because every person between the ages of 13 and 19 has to report to the iTunes Store as part of the government's Selective Service Online Shopping Act of 1984, which stipulates that every male child over the age of 14 must stare directly and blankly into a hand-held video game device for no less than nine hours per day (including a mandatory two hours during school). As I was saying, this chapter is for people who need a quick course on what iTunes is, what's in the iTunes Store (and how to buy stuff there), and then how to get that stuff into their iPhone without any person between the ages of 13 and 19 ever looking up from their screen. This, I think we can do.

Importing Songs from CDs

Chances are if you haven't been using an iPod up to this point, most of your music collection is still on CDs. Luckily, getting them into iTunes (and from there into your iPhone) couldn't be easier. Start by launching iTunes (remember—you have to have at least iTunes version 7.7 or higher to sync with your iPhone. If you don't, go to Apple's website and download the latest version). When iTunes appears, put a music CD into your computer's CD/DVD drive, and a dialog will appear asking if you'd like to import the songs on your CD into your iTunes Music Library. All you have to do is click the Yes button, and iTunes does the rest—importing each song, in order, with the track names—for you. It puts these songs into your Music Library mixed in with all your other songs (see "Creating Music Playlists" on page 144 for how to keep these songs separate).

---

iTip

If you have an Internet connection when you go to import a music CD, iTunes will go to the Web, cross reference the name of your CD with an online music database, and in most cases, it will automatically add the track names to all of your songs. If it couldn't find your CD in its vast database, you must have some mighty obscure musical taste, and I mean that in the most nonjudgmental, totally disingenuous way possible.

Buying Songs from the iTunes Store

You buy iPhone-compatible music from the iTunes Store (the iTunes Store is the single largest online music retailer in the world today) and to enter the store, just click on iTunes Store in the Source list on the left side of the iTunes window. Although you can jump directly to different genres (like Rock, Hip-Hop, Country, Pop, etc.) and browse through there, the quickest way to find the music you want is to do a search using the Search field in the upper-right corner of the iTunes window. Here I entered "Coldplay," then hit the Return (PC: Enter) key on my keyboard, and in just seconds all the Coldplay albums and songs available on iTunes appeared (as seen here). You can buy (and download on the spot) individual songs for 99¢, or an entire album for varying prices (the Coldplay albums go for anywhere from $9.99 to $11.99). To hear a 30-second preview of any song, just double-click on its title. If you want to buy a song, click the Buy Song button (circled above in red), and it's immediately downloaded to your computer (of course, before you can start buying and downloading songs, you'll have to take a moment and create an iTunes account, so do that now. No problem…I'll wait). Okay, so that's pretty much the scoop—you can use the Search field to find just the song(s) you want, or you can click the Home button (that little icon that looks like a house just below the Volume slider on the top-left side), and browse through the iTunes Store's huge collection of songs (there are more than a million). Any songs you buy are added to your Music Library and they'll also appear under Purchased in the Source list.

Creating Music Playlists

So, you've imported some songs from CDs, and you've bought a few songs from the iTunes Store, and they're all there together in your Music Library (if you go to the top of the Source list on the left side of the iTunes window and click on Music, you'll see every song you have in iTunes). The way you keep things organized is by creating playlists, which are basically collections of your favorite songs. So, for example, if you wanted to create a collection of nothing but your favorite songs to listen to in the car, you would start by clicking on the + (plus sign) button at the bottom-left corner of the iTunes window. This adds a new blank playlist to your Source list, and its name is highlighted so you can type in a name (how about "Driving Mix"?). Once you've named your playlist, press the Return (PC: Enter) key on your keyboard to lock in the name of your playlist, then make sure you click on Music in the Source list to show your entire iTunes Music Library of songs. Now, scroll through your music collection and each time you run across one of your favorite driving songs, click-and-drag that song onto your Driving Mix playlist in the Source list. A green circle with a + (plus sign) in it appears to let you know that you're adding a song to that playlist (as seen here). Once you've gone through and added all your driving favorites, you're only one click away from hearing just those songs (and you'll be able to transfer this new playlist to your iPhone). Also, once your songs are in a playlist, you can click-and-drag them into the order you'd like them to appear. To delete a song from a playlist, just click on it and hit the Delete (PC: Backspace) key on your keyboard (this doesn't delete it from your Music Library, just from that playlist).

Creating Smart Playlists

If you don't want to take the time to make a bunch of different playlists (actually, making your own custom playlists is half the fun of using iTunes), you can have iTunes do most of the work for you. iTunes already comes with some of these "Smart Playlists." For example, you'll see playlists already created with the 25 songs you've played the most, the songs you've played most recently, and if you rate your songs in iTunes (using the 1- to 5-star rating system), you'll see only your top-rated songs in a Smart Playlist. To create your own Smart Playlist, just press-and-hold the Option key on a Mac, or the Shift key on a PC, and click the + (plus sign) button at the bottom-left corner of iTunes. This brings up a dialog that asks you to choose the criteria for your new Smart Playlist. So, let's say you've imported three or four different Elvis CDs, and you've bought some Elvis songs from the iTunes Store. When your Smart Playlist dialog appears, you can have it search your entire Music Library and build a playlist of all your Elvis songs for you (as shown above). These Smart Playlists are incredibly powerful, yet easy to use—you just choose your criteria from the pop-up menus. Let's try another: want all of your dance music songs in one playlist? Change the Artist field to Genre, erase "Elvis" and type in "Dance," then click OK. To narrow your criteria even further, click the gray + (plus sign) button to the right of the text field (where you typed "Dance") to add another line of search criteria.

Downloading Radio & Video Podcasts

Podcasts are free radio or TV shows produced by individuals or companies on a wide range of topics, from teaching you how to cook, to teaching you martial arts, to shows that are just comedy, or product reviews, or news. Everyone from ESPN to National Geographic, from HBO to NPR (radio), and about everybody in between offers free downloadable podcasts, which you can subscribe to (for free) and they're downloaded to your computer (and then onto your iPhone, if you choose) as soon as each episode is released (some are daily, some post weekly episodes, some bi-weekly, etc.). To find a podcast that interests you, go to the iTunes Store, and on the homepage click on Podcasts. There are podcasts on the Podcasts main page, and you can search through different categories (like Sports & Recreation, Technology, Health, etc.). When you find one you like, you can click the Get Episode button to download just an episode, or click the Subscribe button to download each episode as they're released for free (you can unsubscribe any time).

---

 iTip

Scott hosts a weekly video podcast called Photoshop User TV *(along with co-hosts Matt Kloskowski and Dave Cross), and each week they share Adobe Photoshop techniques, tips, news, and step-by-step tutorials. Each episode is approximately 30 minutes and they have an awful lot of fun (and millions of downloads each month around the world). You can find it on iTunes by searching for* Photoshop User TV.

Buying TV Shows and Movies

Besides buying music, you can also buy full-length movies, TV shows, and music videos from the iTunes Store and you can watch these on your iPhone, as well. From the iTunes Store homepage, in the navigation list at the top left of the main window, click on either Movies, TV Shows, or Music Videos. When your choice appears, you'll find featured titles. For example, if you chose TV Shows, you would see the entire seasons of TV shows from ABC, NBC, CBS, FOX, and more than 60 broadcast and cable channels (individual episodes cost $1.99 each, but you can buy an entire season of a show—every episode which aired that year—and those prices vary. You can now buy high-definition versions of many shows—they cost $2.99). Movies have their own section on the iTunes Store, as well, and full-length movies run from around $9.99 to $14.99, for the most part. You can also rent movies for $2.99 and $3.99, and you'll have 30 days to enjoy them either on your iPhone, iPod, computer, or Apple TV. Once you start watching a movie rental, you'll have 24 hours to finish it or watch it as many times as you like before it deletes itself.

 iTip

Playlists aren't just for music—you can create your own custom playlists for your favorite TV shows or movies (so you could have a playlist of just scary movies, or a playlist of classic TV shows). You create them just like you would a music playlist.

Choosing What Goes into Your iPhone

Since iPhones don't have as much storage space as your computer does, you wouldn't want to put all of your movies, podcasts, and TV shows onto your iPhone at once (you'd probably run out of room), so iTunes lets you choose which music playlists, which TV shows, and which movies get uploaded. You do this by connecting your iPhone to your computer, and then in iTunes, in the Source list on the left side of the window, click on your iPhone to bring up its preferences in the main window. You'll see a row of tabs along the top of the main window for Music, Photos, Podcasts, Video, etc. For example, click on the Video tab, and when the Video preferences window appears (shown here), in the TV Shows section near the top of the screen, instead of choosing to sync All TV Shows, choose Selected TV Shows instead. Then in the list of TV shows you have in iTunes, only check the shows you want uploaded to your iPhone. You can choose to upload all unwatched shows, or just the three most recent, five most recent, etc. This way you can control which shows, and how many, are uploaded to your iPhone. Once you make your changes, be sure to click the Apply button in the lower-right corner of the iTunes window (it's circled here in red).

Going from iTunes to Your iPhone

Once you've chosen which music playlists, movies, podcasts, music videos, and TV shows in your iTunes preferences to sync to your IPhone, and have synced your iTunes and your iPhone, when you download new ones, all you have to do to get them on your iPhone is to connect your iPhone to your computer. iTunes will automatically launch (once you connect your iPhone) and it will immediately start uploading just the music playlists, videos, movies, podcasts, and TV shows you've chosen in the preferences. That's all there is to it.

---

iTip

We have just scratched the surface of what you can do in iTunes and the iTunes Store. If you're into this kind of stuff, we know a guy who wrote a killer book on iTunes, the iPod, and the iTunes Store. His book is called (ready for this?) The iPod Book (from Peachpit Press), and we have to say, it looks pretty much like this book. In fact, this book is based on the layout and design of that book. But we won't get in trouble because Scott's the author of that book, too! (Aw come on, you knew that was coming, right?)

Buying Custom Ringtones

You can convert many of your favorite purchased songs into ringtones in the iTunes Store for the current rate of 99¢ (see page 222 in Chapter 9 for how to create ringtones from non-iTunes purchased songs). First, you have to determine if the song you want to convert is available as a ringtone. The easiest way to do this is to first turn on the Ringtone column—just click on your Music Library in the Source list on the left side of the iTunes window, then choose View Options from the View menu, turn on the Ringtones checkbox, and click OK. In the dialog that appears, click Check Songs. You'll then see a Ringtone column in your music list—the ringtone icon is a bell. Any songs that have a bell icon next to them are available as ringtones in iTunes. You can convert any of these songs by clicking on the bell icon to bring up the iTunes Ringtone Editor at the bottom of the window. You can select which portion of the song you want to be a ringtone, up to 30 seconds worth—the default is 15 seconds. You can move the blue area to any part of the song you want to be part of the ringtone by just clicking-and-dragging on its outer edges, and also have it fade in and fade out. Click the Preview button near the bottom of the window to listen to your selection. Once you're satisfied with the area you selected, you can click the Buy button to buy it and it will be converted and added to your Ringtones Library. The next time you sync your iPhone, it will be transferred over (if you have this preference set) and available as a ringtone to assign to a contact(s) or to be used as your default ringtone.

Using the iTunes Wi-Fi Music Store

You don't have to wait until you're back at your home or office to buy that tune you just heard. If you have a Wi-Fi connection, you can buy songs from iTunes right from your iPhone. Tap the iTunes button on your Home screen to be taken to the iTunes Store. From there, you'll be able to access the millions of songs available on iTunes. You can browse the Featured or Top Tens lists, or you can just search for the exact song, artist, or album you're looking for. Once you find a song, you can tap it to play a preview of it or double-tap on it to view the entire album. If you decide to buy a song, just tap the price button next to the song you want to purchase. It will change from the price to a Buy Now button. Tap the Buy Now button, and you'll then be prompted to enter your iTunes account username and password to complete the purchase. Once you enter your information, your song will be downloaded and available for playback in your iPod application. The next time you sync your iPhone with your computer, the songs you purchased will be synced to your computer (if you have this preference set).

 iTip

If you've got an iTunes gift card or other iTunes certificate, you can redeem them directly in the iTunes Store on your iPhone. Just tap the Downloads button and then tap the Redeem button at the top left of the screen. You can then key in the access code from the gift card and the card's value will be added to your account immediately.

Getting Third-Party Apps from the iTunes App Store

There are hundreds of third-party applications available for the iPhone, with hundreds more on the way. You can get games, utilities, social networking apps—you name it. These applications are available exclusively through the iTunes Store's App Store. Many of them are available free of charge, and the vast majority of those that cost money are under $10. To see the available applications, you'll need iTunes version 7.7 or later. On your computer, you can click the App Store link on the left side of the iTunes Store's homepage. This will take you to the various listings of iPhone applications. You can also do searches using the Search field at the top right of the window, just like you do for songs. Once you find an application that you want to download and use, you can click on it and then click the Buy App button (or the Get App button, if it's free). You'll see the price right next to the application and, again, many of them are free. Your application(s) will be downloaded to your computer and appear in your Applications Library in the Source list. The next time you sync your iPhone, your new application(s) will be installed on it (if you have that preference set). You can then access them on your Home screen and enjoy the benefits that they offer.

Getting Third-Party Apps from the iPhone App Store

If you have a Wi-Fi connection, you can also get applications for your iPhone directly on your iPhone, as Apple has included an iPhone version of the App Store. Just tap the App Store button on your Home screen and you'll be connected to the same App Store as if you were doing it via iTunes, however, this App Store is formatted specifically for your iPhone. You can browse the Featured applications, or you can look through the Categories, or check out the Top 25 applications. If you know the name of the application you're looking for, you can tap Search and key in the name of the application to search for it. Once you find an application you want to download to your iPhone, just tap the price (or Free) button, then tap the Buy Now (or Install) button, and you'll be prompted to enter your iTunes username and password. The application will then be downloaded and installed directly on your iPhone. The next time you sync your iPhone with your computer, the application will be downloaded to your iTunes Applications Library (if you have that preference set).

---

iTip

Have a neat idea for an iPhone app? Just contact the folks at DS Media Labs, Inc. (www.dsmedialabs.com). We'd like to thank Ben Stahlhood, who is currently developing an iPhone app for us right now!

Updating Your Apps in iTunes

Just like any other software application out there, iPhone applications will be updated from time to time. To check to see if your applications have any available updates, just open iTunes on your computer and click on your Applications Library in the Source list on the left side of the window. Then, click the Check for Updates link in the bottom-right corner of the iTunes window, and if there are any updates available, you'll be taken to a screen that lists them, where you can then update your applications individually or all at once. Once the update process is complete, you'll still need to sync your iPhone to your computer in order to get the updates installed on your iPhone.

Updating Your Apps on the iPhone

You can also get your iPhone application updates directly on your iPhone. Just tap the App Store button on your Home screen and you'll see an Updates button in the lower-right corner. Tap the Updates button to see if any of your installed applications have updates. If they do, you'll be able to update them directly from the screen that comes up.

Deleting Third-Party Apps from iTunes

At some point, you may decide that the really cool application you downloaded a month ago really isn't that cool after all, or you may find a better one. If you decide that you no longer want a particular application, just click on its icon in your Applications Library in iTunes and hit the Delete (PC: Backspace) key on your keyboard. You'll then be prompted by a warning letting you know that if you delete the app from iTunes, it will also be deleted from your iPhone the next time you sync. Click the Remove button and the next dialog will ask if you want to move the application to the Trash (PC: Recycle Bin). Click the Move to Trash (PC: Move to Recycle Bin) button and the next time you empty the Trash, the application will be deleted from your computer. Also, the next time you sync your iPhone, the application will be uninstalled from your iPhone (if you have that preference set).

Deleting Third–Party Apps from the iPhone

If you want to delete a third-party application that is installed on your iPhone, on the Home screen, tap-and-hold your finger on the application you want to remove. All of your icons will start to wiggle and you'll see an X appear in the upper-left corner of each third-party application. Tap the X to remove the application from your Home screen and your iPhone. The next time you sync your iPhone, the application will also be removed from iTunes (if you have that preference set).

One of the Coolest Apps

There are tons of cool applications in the App Store and I could go on and on about them, but one of the coolest is from Apple, and it's free! It's called Remote, and it turns your iPhone into a Wi-Fi remote for your iTunes applications running on your computer or your Apple TV. Although the above iPhone screen capture (on the right) looks like the iPod application on the iPhone at first glance, it's actually my iMac running iTunes in the next room. I'm able to navigate all the music on the iMac (or PC) and select which playlists to play. I can advance or rewind songs. I can even control which (AirTunes) speakers the music will play through. If you have an Apple TV, it gets even better. You get all the same controls, however, your iPhone onscreen keyboard becomes the keyboard to your Apple TV, which comes in real handy for keying in searches. Did I mention that this app is *free*? You can download it right now from the App Store on your iPhone, or through iTunes on your computer. If you have iTunes on your computer (and if you have an iPhone, you do) and a Wi-Fi network, this is a must-have application!

Creating Genius Playlists in iTunes

iTunes 8 includes an incredible new feature that creates a playlist based on one song you choose and other songs you have in your Music Library that are similar or would go well with it. Once you install iTunes 8 (or higher), choose Turn On Genius from the Store menu. iTunes then will send an anonymous snapshot of your Music Library up to "the clouds" (Apple's iTunes servers) and it will be combined with Music Library lists from other users to create more accurate Genius playlists based on the songs you choose. Once you have the Genius feature turned on, all you have to do is choose a song in your Music Library and click the Genius button in the bottom right-hand corner, and iTunes will build a new playlist of up to 25 songs that should go well with the song you initially selected. You can choose between 25, 50, 75, and 100 songs from the Limit To pop-up menu at the top of the main iTunes window. You can also click the Save Playlist button at the top if you want to keep it and use it again in the future, or click the Refresh button to see if the Genius feature makes an even better playlist (this will be more helpful if you save the playlist and refresh it later, after you've added more songs and Apple has gathered more information). By default, your iTunes Genius information will be updated weekly, so that your Genius playlists get even smarter.

Chapter Seven

Video Killed
the Radio Star

Using the iPhone's
Built-In iPod

 It's hard to believe, but the 1979 song "Video Killed the Radio Star," from The Buggles, actually has an important place in music history because when MTV went live back in August 1981, their debut music video was (you guessed it) "Video Killed the Radio Star." I have a regular iPod that does play video, but it doesn't have the larger, more luxurious widescreen display the iPhone has, and it was while pondering that thought, I realized the iPhone itself was playing a role in music history, and as an iPhone owner, like MTV, I would have to choose which music video would debut on my iPhone. Knowing that my choice would, in some small way, be part of my own personal music history really put a lot of pressure on me. I mean, think about it—years from now, it's quite possible that sociology students at colleges in far off places, like Helsinki and Cincinnati, might one day study, debate, and pick apart my music video debut choice, and I'm not sure I can deal with that kind of responsibility. And that's probably why, when I was carefully scrolling through my music video collection, rather than "flicking" or "swiping," I accidentally tapped the Play button right when the Spice Girls' "Wannabe" video was scrolling by, and I swear it felt like I went into some kind of slow motion dream state as I scrambled and fumbled to tap the Pause button…but it was too late. There it was, playing full screen. My only solace was, like The Buggles, the Spice Girls are British. If you listen carefully, you can almost hear the university professors in Helsinki giggling as they type their fall course descriptions.

Syncing Your iTunes Library

When you connected your iPhone to set it up and activate it, you had preference tabs in iTunes for Music, Podcasts, Video, etc. These tabs allow you to control which songs, playlists, podcasts, videos, etc., get synced to your iPhone. Since the iPhone has limited capacity, it is quite common to have more content on your computer than your iPhone will hold. Therefore, it's best to create playlists and rules for how things get synced to your iPhone. If you haven't already, create some playlists of your favorite tunes—the ones that you'll really want to listen to while you're on the go (this is covered in detail in the iTunes chapter of this book). When it comes to podcasts and videos, you can not only specify which shows/movies get synced to your iPhone, but you can also specify things like only sync unwatched episodes or the most recent ones. When you watch them on your iPhone, the next time you sync your iPhone to your computer, iTunes will mark them as watched and sync the next most recent or unwatched episodes. Once you change your settings in iTunes for what will be synced with your iPhone (by clicking on a tab, turning on the Sync option, and choosing your settings), you can click the Apply button to save the settings and initiate an immediate sync.

Launching the iPod Application

Unlike other iPods you may have used, the iPod on the iPhone is an application. To launch it, from the Home screen, tap the iPod button. This will take you to the iPod application, which will allow you to play your music and video files that you synced from iTunes. Although you launch the iPod application, you don't have to stay in it just to listen to your content. Once you start a song, podcast, or audiobook playing, you can switch to other iPhone applications, such as Mail or Safari, and the iPod will keep playing your audio.

Navigating the iPod

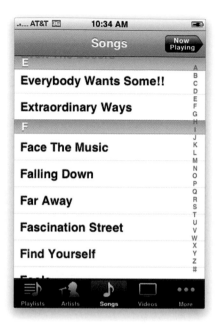

By default, when you launch the iPod application on the iPhone, at the bottom of the screen you will have buttons for Playlists, Artists, Songs, Videos, and More. These buttons allow you direct access to those areas. You can jump back and forth between these areas at any time to access your content in the way that you want. You'll likely use Playlists most often. However, if you've got a tune stuck in your head and you want to play it immediately, then you could tap the Songs button and go right to your list of songs. Since it is possible to have literally thousands of songs on your iPhone, the list could be quite long. You can jump to a specific letter of the alphabet by tapping on the letter you want to jump to along the right edge of the list.

---

iTip

If you want to see how many songs you have on your iPhone, tap the Songs button and scroll down to the bottom of the list. You can see your song count listed there.

Playing Your First Song on the iPhone

If you're like me, you'll want to check out the iPod application on the iPhone pretty quickly. So tap the iPod button on the Home screen and then either tap Playlists, Artists, or Songs to find the first song that you would like to hear. Once you locate your song, just tap it to begin playing it. Since the iPhone has a built-in speaker, you'll actually hear the sound come from the iPhone's speaker if you don't have headphones plugged in. If the song has album art, it will be displayed while the song plays. If there is no album art, then the iPhone will just display a default music note while the song plays. If you want to pick a different song, you don't have to stop or pause the current song. Just tap the left arrow button in the upper-left corner of the iPod screen to return to your Songs list. Once your song finishes, the iPhone will automatically play the next song in the list. To conserve battery life, the iPhone's display will go to sleep while the song is playing. To get back to the iPod, just press the Home button and unlock the iPhone by swiping your finger across to the right on the Slide to Unlock button.

Adjusting the Volume

There are two ways to adjust the playback volume on the iPhone. The first way is using the onscreen volume slider that is at the bottom of the iPod screen. Just use your finger to drag the knob (circle) to the right to make the playback louder or to the left to lower the volume. The other way to adjust the volume is to use the physical volume buttons on the left side of the iPhone. These are the same buttons that you use to adjust the ringer volume and call volume, too.

Using Your Playlists

The idea of playlists is what separated the iPod from most other MP3 players back in 2001. So it's only natural that the iPhone would have great playlist support. Playlists are created on your computer in iTunes. You can pick and choose which playlists get synced to your iPhone from iTunes. Once you go to the iPod application from the Home screen, you will have a Playlists button. Tap this button to see your available playlists on the iPhone. When you tap on any of your playlists, you'll see the songs contained in that playlist. Tapping any song will begin playing that song. The subsequent songs in the playlist will play in order. The great part about playlists is that you can have as many as you want with no real storage penalty. The same song(s) can be in multiple playlists but not take up additional space on the iPhone. For example, let's say you have a playlist called Male Vocals and one called Quiet Storm. Both playlists could contain John Mayer's "Say" track. However, that track will only be copied to the iPhone once, no matter how many playlists it's in. So go nuts creating any playlists that might suit your mood at any given time.

Shuffle Your Songs

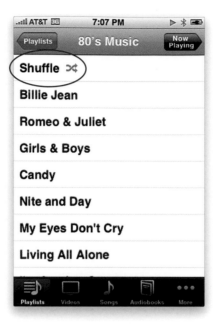

It's great to be able to listen to your songs in the order that you placed them in your playlist. However, it's often more fun to let fate decide which song is going to play next. This way you're constantly surprised because you don't know what's coming next. You can play your songs in order by tapping on any song in any playlist. However, if you want the songs in a particular playlist to play randomly, tap Shuffle at the top of the playlist instead. Shuffle will be at the top of any playlist of songs that contains two or more songs. This will pick the first song at random and play the rest of the playlist in random order.

Playing Songs by Artist

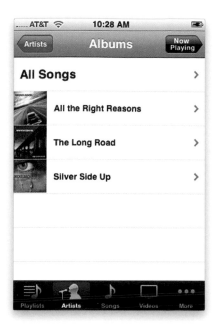

I'm in the mood to hear some Nickelback, but I didn't create a specific playlist to hear their music. No worries. The iPod application on the iPhone lets you play songs by specific artists. From the iPod's main screen, tap the Artists button. You will then see a list of all your artists. From this list, you can tap the specific artist that you want to hear. Then you'll see a choice between All Songs and the individual albums that you have from that artist. (*Note:* If you only have one album from that artist, then you'll just see the songs.) You'll see this list of albums even if you don't have all the songs on any of the given albums. You can now either tap All Songs to see a list of all the songs you have by that artist or you can tap a specific album to just play the songs on that album. Either way, you'll be able to play the songs in order or tap Shuffle (provided you have two or more songs) to play the songs at random.

Fast Forward or Rewind Through a Song

There are some songs that you can listen to over and over again and never get tired of them. However, there are some songs that you can listen to a certain part of the song over and over again, or there's a certain part of the song that you can't stand. Either way, there is a way to "scrub" through a song that is playing. Of course, in order for this to work, you have to start a song playing. So tap the iPod button on the Home screen, choose a song by playlist, artist, or song and start playing it by tapping on it. You will either see the album art for the song, or a music note if there is no album art for that song. In either case, tap the screen right on the artwork. This will display a progress bar at the top of the screen. As the song plays, the little knob on the progress bar will be advancing to the right. You can tap right on that knob and drag it left to go back in the song or right to move forward through the song. Tap the artwork again to hide the progress bar.

Repeating Playback of a Song or Playlist

If you want to hear the same playlist or song over and over again, you can turn on the Repeat feature in the iPod application. Start playing the song that you want to repeat or a song from the playlist that you want to repeat. Tap on the album art and you'll notice a little circular arrow button to the left of the progress bar. This allows you to turn on Repeat. There are three modes to Repeat: Tapping the Repeat button once will repeat the entire playlist after all the songs have been played. Tapping the Repeat button again will show the circular arrow Repeat button with a 1 on it. This means that the current song will repeat over and over until you stop it. Tapping the Repeat button one more time will turn Repeat off.

Advancing to the Next Song

You can advance to the next song by tapping the double arrows that point to the right beneath the album art of the currently playing song. You can also go to the previous song by tapping the double arrows that point to the left. However, there's an even cooler way to advance to the next song. The iPhone comes with a pair of earbuds that also double as a hands-free headset for making calls. There is a little microphone on the right earbud cable. That microphone is also a button that will advance to the next song while you're listening to music on your iPhone. To advance to the next song, press this button (squeeze it) twice quickly.

Pausing Playback

Although you're in the groove now, you will want to be able to pause the iPod playback from time to time. The good news is that there are a few ways to do this: First off, if you receive a call, the iPhone will automatically pause the iPod playback until you complete your call, and then pick right back up where you left off. The second way to pause playback is to do so right on the iPod screen. Tap the Pause button at the bottom of the screen. Lastly, if you're listening to your content with the supplied Apple iPhone headset, you can press the microphone button once to pause playback. To resume playback, just press the button again.

Using Cover Flow

Cover Flow gives you a visual organic way of flipping through your music collection. This feature first appeared in iTunes 7 and the iPhone's iPod application was the first iPod to get this feature. To use Cover Flow, tap on the iPod button on the Home screen. Once you're in the iPod application, simply hold up your iPhone and rotate it 90° in either direction. This will automatically switch the display to Cover Flow. You will now see your album art (or the music symbol). You can flick or drag your finger across the screen to move through your albums. Once you find an album that you're interested in drilling down further on, you can tap it and it will flip over to reveal the songs on that album. You can tap any song to play it. The playback will be limited to the songs on that particular album. You can flip the album back over again by tapping the name of the album at the top.

---

iTip

You can also flip albums over and back by tapping the little "i" button in the lower-right corner of the Cover Flow screen.

Playing Other Songs from the Same Album

While it's great to be able to access all the songs of a particular album while you're in Cover Flow view, you can also access songs from the same album as the song that is currently playing. Start any song playing in the iPod application that has at least two songs from the same album. Now tap the little Track list button in the top-right corner of the screen (to the right of the song's name). This will flip the album over and reveal the other songs that are on that album. You can start playing any song you want on that list without having to go find it elsewhere.

Rating Your Songs on the iPhone

iTunes has some really slick features that take advantage of song ratings. For example, you can create Smart Playlists that contain your top-rated tunes (see Chapter 6 for more on Smart Playlists). While it's great that you can rate the songs as 1- to 5-star right in iTunes, it's sometimes more convenient to rate songs right on your iPhone while you're out and about. The next time you sync your iPhone to iTunes, the ratings you made on the iPhone will be applied to your songs in iTunes (if you have this preference set). To rate any song that is currently playing, tap the Track list button above the upper-right corner of the album art. The album art will flip over and you will see either five dots or the current rating that the song has. You can then tap the appropriate star/dot to rate your song as 1- to 5-star. Once you're done rating it, just tap the little Album Art button in the upper-right corner to return to your album art display.

Sing Along with the Lyrics

iTunes supports having the actual lyrics to your songs embedded in the song files them-selves. If you've taken the time to find the lyrics to your favorite songs, you can paste them into the Lyrics section for that particular song (by clicking on the song in your Music Library, choosing Get Info from the File menu, and then clicking on the Lyrics tab). The next time you sync your iPhone, the updated song will be downloaded to it with the lyrics (if you have this preference set). To display the lyrics of a song that is playing on your iPhone, simply tap the album art that is currently displaying. To hide the lyrics again, just tap the lyrics, and they will go away and the album art will be displayed again.

Taking Advantage of Podcasts

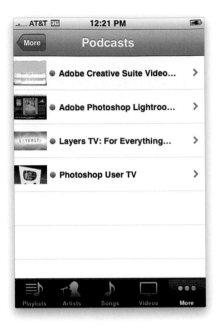

Podcasts are a great way to keep up on the topics that you're interested in while you're on the go. There is a huge library of both audio and video podcasts in the iTunes Store, and the best part is that they are usually *free* to subscribe to. You can watch or listen to podcasts right in iTunes, but more importantly, you can watch or listen to them on your iPhone. Once you've downloaded or subscribed to a podcast or two, you can then choose to have those episodes sync to your iPhone from iTunes. Once you have some podcast episodes on your iPhone, you can get to them from the iPod application. Tap the More button on the bottom-right side of the iPod screen and then tap Podcasts. You'll see your podcasts listed by show, and from there you can tap on a particular show to choose an episode to listen to. Tap it and away you go. If you listen to it all the way through, the next time you sync to iTunes, it will mark it as heard and therefore remove it from the iPhone, or it will remember where you left off.

---

iTip

Hey, if you're looking for a couple of great podcasts to subscribe to, check out Scott's Photoshop User TV *and Terry's* Adobe Creative Suite Video Podcast: *www.photoshop-usertv.com and www.creativesuitepodcast.com. You can subscribe to both of these video podcasts for free right in iTunes.*

Watching Videos and Movies on the iPhone

Apple has done a good job supporting video playback on the iPhone. Using the iPod application, you can watch movies, music videos, and TV shows that you purchase from iTunes *or* ones that you create yourself. You can also watch video podcasts and iTunes movie rentals. To watch a video, tap the Videos button at the bottom of the iPod screen. Your video content will be organized by Movies, TV Shows, Music Videos, and Podcasts. Tap the video you want to play and it automatically plays horizontally—just rotate your iPhone to watch it and it plays full screen. You can access the playback controls while it's playing by just tapping the screen. There are two screen modes: full screen and wide-screen. To toggle between them, double-tap the screen. In widescreen mode, you'll see the entire video from edge to edge. If the video is at a different aspect ratio, then it may be presented with black bars at the top and bottom or left and right. You can also play it full screen so that there are no bars, but some of the video may be cropped off.

> **iTip**
>
> *You can convert your home movies into the proper format right in iTunes. Add the movie to iTunes and choose Create iPod or iPhone Version from the Advanced menu. Another hot tip: You can delete videos directly from the iPhone to make more room. Tap the Videos button and flick your finger across the title of the video to expose the Delete button. Tap Delete to delete the video from the iPhone immediately.*

Enjoying iTunes Movie Rentals

You can also watch movies you've rented from iTunes on your iPhone. Unlike other movies in your iTunes Movies Library, iTunes movie rentals aren't automatically synced to your iPhone (if you have your iPhone set to automatically sync). Instead, you have to select them and manually sync them from your iTunes Movies Library to your iPhone. To rent a movie and take it with you on your iPhone, click on iTunes Store in the Source list on the left side of the iTunes window, go to Movies in the iTunes Store, and rent the movie of your choice. Once it downloads, you can connect your iPhone to your computer and select your iPhone in the Source list. You'll see all your rented movies in the Video tab of the iPhone preferences that appear in the main iTunes window. Click on the Move button next to each movie you rented and want to sync to your iPhone, then click the Apply button at the bottom-right of the window. Your computer will need to be connected to the Internet at the time you do the sync. Once you sync your rental(s) to your iPhone, it is removed from your iTunes Movies Library, and you'll have 30 days to watch the rental(s) before it automatically deletes itself from your iPhone. Once you start watching an iTunes movie rental, you'll have 24 hours to finish watching it. You can watch it as many times as you want within that 24-hour period, though. After the 24 hours is up, the movie will automatically be deleted from your iPhone.

Audiobooks

Audiobooks are great to listen to on the go. Unlike songs, the iPhone remembers where you left off, whether you started listening to the audiobook in iTunes or on your iPhone. Therefore, you can feel free to listen in either place and the next time you sync to your computer, iTunes will update the audiobook to remember where you left off (if you have this preference set). The iTunes Store has a wide variety of audiobook choices. To listen to an audiobook on your iPhone, tap the More button at the bottom of the iPod screen, then tap Audiobooks. Tap the audiobook you want to listen to, to begin playback. The Next/Fast Forward and Previous/Rewind buttons will advance to the next chapter or go back to the previous chapter.

Create an On-The-Go Playlist

At some point, you may want to create a playlist while you're away from your computer. The songs are already on your iPhone, but you want to put them in a particular order right then and there. The iPhone supports creating playlists on the fly. They're called On-The-Go playlists. To create an On-The-Go playlist, tap the Playlists button at the bottom of the iPod screen. The first item in the list is the On-The-Go playlist option. Once you tap it, you'll be presented with a list of all your songs. Each song will have a + (plus sign) to the right of it. You can just tap the plus sign for each song that you want to add to the On-The-Go playlist. As you tap each song, it will gray out to indicate that it has been added. When you're done adding songs, tap the Done button and your new On-The-Go playlist will be ready for use. If you want to edit it, you can tap the Edit button in the top-right corner of the On-The-Go playlist screen. You can then change the order of the songs by tapping-and-dragging the triple-line icon to the right of the song you want to move, or you can delete songs from the list by tapping the little red circle on the left side of the song and then tapping the Delete button. You can also add additional songs by tapping the + (plus sign) button in the top-left corner of the screen. When you're done editing, tap the Done button in the top-right corner of the screen.

Receiving a Call While Listening to the iPod

SCOTT KELBY

Apple did a great job of integrating the Phone application with the iPod application. When you receive a call, the music will fade and you'll hear your phone ring. The iPhone will give you the choice of answering the call or declining it (which will send the caller to voicemail). If you answer the call, then you'll be taken to the iPhone's call screen. Once you end the call, the iPhone will pick up right where it left off playing your song or other media.

iTip

If you're listening to the iPod via the supplied stereo headset, you can also answer the call by clicking the microphone button on the right headset cable.

Controlling Your iPod
While You're in Another App

Once you start a song or playlist going in your iPod app, you can leave the app by clicking the Home button. The music will keep playing and you can then launch another app, such as the Weather app. However, if you want to control your iPod while you're in another app, you don't have to go back to the iPod app to do so. All you have to do is double-click the Home button. This will bring up the iPod controls and overlay them on top of the app you're currently in. Once the controls appear, you can pause the song, advance to the next song, go back to the previous song, control the volume, or tap the iPod button to return to the iPod app. Once you're done with the onscreen controls, you can just tap the Close button to return to the app you are in. Also note that the default behavior for double-clicking the Home button is to take you to your phone Favorites list. However, if you have music playing, the default is to bring up the iPod controls instead.

---

iTip

If all you want to do is control the volume, you don't have to bring up the iPod controls. You can use the up and down buttons on the left side of the iPhone to control your iPod volume while a song is playing.

Using External Speakers or Headsets

Since the iPhone has a great iPod built into it, it stands to reason that you may want to connect your iPhone to some speakers to get the party rolling. The iPhone does have a standard 30-pin iPod dock connector on the bottom of it. It also has a stereo headphone jack on the top, but there are some caveats. Since the iPhone is a GSM-based phone, its built-in "radio" could interfere with your stereo or speakers. When you plug your iPhone into a speaker system built for the iPod (not for the iPhone), you may get a message that says "This accessory is not made to work with iPhone. Would you like to turn on Airplane Mode to reduce audio interference (you will not be able to make or receive calls)?" You have the choice of turning on Airplane mode or not. What this simply means is that while in Airplane mode, the phone and Bluetooth portions of the iPhone are turned off, so as not to interfere with your stereo speakers. However, while in Airplane mode you will not be able to make or receive calls. So you might want to try it on your speakers without going into Airplane mode. If there is no interference, you're home free. You can also use the iPhone Dock (available at the Apple Store). It has a stereo line out port that can be used to connect directly to your stereo system. If you want to use your own headphones you can, but there may be an issue actually plugging them in. The iPhone's headset jack is recessed and therefore your headset plug may not be skinny enough to fit down in there. Luckily, Belkin, Monster, and Griffin Technologies have made adapters.

Setting a Sleep Timer

You can actually have your iPhone's music lull you off to sleepy land by setting a sleep timer. A sleep timer will play your music until the timer expires and then it will put the iPhone to sleep. To set a sleep timer, first go to your iPod application and start playing the songs you want to play until the timer goes off. You can use a playlist (such as your "sleepy land" playlist—I know you have one—or any other playlist on your iPhone). Then press the Home button to go to the Home screen. Now tap Clock and then tap Timer. You can set the minutes, or hours and minutes, that you want the iPod to play before going to sleep. Next tap the When Timer Ends button and choose Sleep iPod. Then tap the Set button in the upper-right corner of the screen to return to the Timer screen. Now tap Start to begin the countdown. When the timer reaches the end of its set time, the music will fade and the iPhone will go to sleep.

Rearranging Your iPod Buttons

The first time you go to the iPod application you'll see buttons at the bottom of the screen for Playlists, Artists, Songs, Videos, and More. When you tap the More button, you'll see that you have a lot more options, such as Albums, Audiobooks, Compilations, Composers, Genres, and Podcasts. However, if you use any of these more often than the default buttons on the main iPod screen, you can swap them. For example, I rarely use the Songs button, but I use the Podcasts button all the time. So rather than having to keep pressing the More button to get to Podcasts, I put the Podcasts button in place of the Songs button. To move a button from the More screen to the main iPod screen, tap the Edit button in the upper-left corner of the More screen. You'll then see icons for all the iPod categories. Simply drag the icon you want to move over the top of the button at the bottom that you want to replace with it, and when the existing button highlights, you can let go. You can tap Done when you've completed your edits.

iTip
While you're choosing which buttons you want to be your primary iPod buttons, you can also drag the ones that are there in a different order. For example, on my iPhone they are now listed as Playlists, Artists, Videos, Podcasts, and More. In the Configure screen, simply drag them in the order you want them listed.

Syncing Your iPhone with Another Computer

If you have your music on one computer and your contacts and calendar on another, you'll be happy to know that the iPhone does sync to more than one computer. For example, I work primarily on my MacBook Pro notebook. However, I have a desktop iMac that serves as our media jukebox. So I sync my contacts, calendars, bookmarks, email accounts, applications, and photos from my MacBook Pro and my music, videos, ringtones, audiobooks, and podcasts from the iMac. Here's how to do it: Sync the iPhone first to the computer that has your data on it—in other words, your contacts, calendars, etc. Uncheck all the things in the Music, Podcasts, Ringtones, and Video tabs (photos and applications can be synced from either computer). Once the sync is done from the first computer, then head over to the other computer (Mac or PC) and launch iTunes. Don't plug in the iPhone just yet. After iTunes is up and running, then go to the iTunes preferences (under the iTunes menu on a Mac or the Edit menu on a PC), click on the Devices icon, turn on the Disable Automatic Syncing for iPhones and iPods checkbox, and click OK. Now you can plug in your iPhone to this computer and when it shows up in the Source list, you can uncheck all the data stuff and enable syncing of all the media stuff. Once you've got the appropriate boxes turned on, you can then hit the Apply button in iTunes to sync your media. From now on, the iPhone will sync data from the first computer and media from the second computer. *Note:* All media has to come from the same computer. Media includes: music, videos, movies, ringtones, podcasts, and audiobooks.

Connect Your iPhone to Your TV

You can enjoy your movies, TV shows, podcasts, and music videos on the big screen. All you need is either the Apple Component AV Cable or the Apple Composite AV Cable. The Apple Composite AV cable is for connecting to TVs (or projectors) with standard RCA-styled connectors—yellow for video, and red and white for stereo audio. However, if you have a newer TV (or HD projector), chances are it has component jacks on the back, which would be red, green, and blue, as well as red and white stereo inputs. So, make sure you check out your TV to see which connections it has before buying your cable. Also note that included with these cables is an additional AC-to-USB adapter, so you'll have power to your iPhone while it's playing. This way you can just leave the cable connected to your TV at all times if you like. Once you have the cable, just tap Settings from your iPhone's Home screen and then tap iPod. If you scroll down to the bottom of the iPod screen, you'll see your options for TV Out. You can have the iPhone display the appropriate format by turning Widescreen on, if you have a 16:9 widescreen TV, and choose between NTSC or PAL, depending upon the standard supported in your country. Once you've chosen the appropriate settings, tap the Home button, and then tap the iPod app. Navigate to the video you want to watch. Connect the cable to your TV and iPhone, and make sure your TV is on the appropriate input for either your composite or component connection. You should then be able to start your video and see it on the big screen. Also, while your movie or video is playing, your iPhone serves as a remote that allows you to pause, skip chapters, etc.

Creating Genius Playlists on Your iPhone

With the iPhone software version 2.1 or higher, you can now have the iPod app create a playlist based on similar songs to the one you choose. In order to use this feature, you must be using the iPhone software version 2.1 or higher and you must have the Genius feature turned on in iTunes 8 or higher. Once you sync your iPhone to your computer with the Genius feature enabled, you'll be able to create Genius playlists directly on your iPhone. Tap the iPod app and then tap Playlists. You'll see the Genius feature at the top. When you tap on Genius, you'll be prompted with a list of your songs to choose from. Once you choose a song, the Genius feature will build a playlist of similar songs and immediately start playing the song you chose. To see the rest of the songs it put in your Genius playlist, tap the left-facing arrow at the top left of your screen. While on this Genius screen, you can just continue to listen to the playlist, or if you really like it, you can save it for later use by tapping the Save button in the top-right corner. To refresh your Genius playlist, tap the Refresh button at the top of the playlist, or you can have it create a new Genius playlist by tapping the New button at the top of the playlist. You can also build a Genius playlist from a song that is currently playing. Just tap the album art and the Genius icon will appear below the progress bar at the top of the screen. Once you tap the Genius icon, it will build a new playlist based on the song that is playing. Genius!

Chapter Eight
One Hour Photo
Enjoying Photos on Your iPhone

I chose the movie *One Hour Photo* as this chapter's title after realizing that my song title choices were pretty much either "Photos of Toast" by Ectogram or "Photos of Nothing" by Southeast Engine. I was leaning towards "Photos of Toast" until I heard "Photos of Nothing," and I knew right then I needed to find something more productive to do for a living other than searching the iTunes Store for songs that contain the word "photo." But I digress. I could have gone with two more obvious choices like "Photograph" from Ringo Starr or Def Leppard. Personally, I like Def Leppard's "Photograph," because I feel cooler lip syncing to them whilst holding a pool cue than I do when singing Ringo's song, which you want to avoid doing in any bar that has a pool table. Luckily that's not a big fear of mine because the odds of finding a jukebox with Ringo's "Photograph" on it (the one that starts with "Every time I see your face, it reminds me of the places we used to go. But all I've got is a photograph...") are less than winning the Powerball lottery. That's because Ringo just isn't very big with the pool hall crowd, which is by the way, a crowd that does favor Def Leppard for one simple reason: Def Leppard is in the Pool Cue Air Guitar Hall of Fame. Sadly, it wasn't for "Photograph"—it was for "Pour Some Sugar On Me," which would have made a great chapter name if the iPhone had either Pouring or Sugar Dispensing features. Sadly, it has neither. I know what you're thinking, "He should have gone with 'Photos of Toast'." That's not what you were thinking, was it?

Getting Photos into Your iPhone (Mac)

If you're using a Mac, the easiest way to get photos into your iPhone is using Apple's iPhoto application (which comes preinstalled on all Macs). You drag-and-drop your photos right onto the iPhoto icon in your Mac's onscreen Dock and it imports them into your iPhoto Library. Then, click on the + (plus sign) button on the bottom left to create separate photo albums (like one for family shots, or one for travel photos, one for your portfolio if you're a serious photographer, etc.), and drag-and-drop photos from the Library right onto the album of your choice. Once your photos are arranged in albums within iPhoto, when you connect your iPhone to your computer, it automatically uploads your photo albums to your iPhone (if you have that preference set). You can see your uploaded albums by starting at the Home screen and tapping on the Photos button in the top row.

iTip

You can set up your iPhone so only certain iPhoto albums are uploaded to it. You do this when your iPhone is connected to your computer, which launches iTunes. Once iTunes is open, on the left side, under Devices, click on the iPhone to bring up the iPhone preferences. Click on the Photos tab, and you'll see that the default setting has all of your iPhoto albums being uploaded. If you'd like to choose just specific albums to be uploaded, click on the Selected Albums radio button and then turn on the checkboxes beside the albums you want uploaded. When you've got just the ones you want uploaded turned on, click the Apply button in the bottom-right corner of iTunes.

Importing Without iPhoto (Mac)

If you don't want to use Apple's iPhoto application to manage the photos you want uploaded to your iPhone, you can just put them in a folder on your Mac and have iTunes do the uploading for you. Here's how: First, connect your iPhone to your computer, which brings up iTunes. In the Source list on the left side of the iTunes window, under Devices, click on your iPhone to bring up the iPhone preferences, then click on the Photos tab. At the top of this window, it says Sync Photos From, and from this pop-up menu, select Choose Folder. This brings up a standard Open dialog, where you choose which folder your photos are in. Once you navigate your way to that folder, click the Choose button, then go to the bottom-right corner of the iTunes window and click the Apply button to upload the photos in that folder to your iPhone. If you have photos in subfolders, they will show up as individual albums on your iPhone, and you can choose which of these subfolders are uploaded by clicking on the Selected Folders radio button and turning on the checkboxes for only the subfolders you want on your iPhone. Easy enough.

Getting Photos into Your iPhone (PC)

There is no version of Apple's iPhoto application for Windows, but luckily it supports direct automatic importing from two other photo management applications: (1) Adobe Photoshop Album (which is a free application—you can download it from www.adobe.com/products/photoshopalbum/starter.html). Or (2) any version of Adobe Photoshop Elements since version 3. To set this up, first connect your iPhone to your computer, which brings up iTunes. In the Source list on the left side of the iTunes window, under Devices, click on your iPhone to bring up the iPhone preferences, then click on the Photos tab. At the top of this window, it says Sync Photos From, and from this pop-up menu, choose which one of the two supported applications you want to import from—Photoshop Album or Photoshop Elements (3 or higher). Now click the Apply button in the bottom-right corner to upload the photos to your iPhone.

Importing Without Album or Elements (PC)

If you don't want to use Photoshop Album or Photoshop Elements to manage the photos you want uploaded to your iPhone, you can just put them in a folder on your PC and have iTunes do the uploading for you. Here's how: First, connect your iPhone to your computer, which brings up iTunes. In the Source list on the left side of the iTunes window, under Devices, click on your iPhone to bring up the iPhone preferences, then click on the Photos tab. At the top of this window, it says Sync Photos From, and from this pop-up menu, select Choose Folder. This brings up a standard Open dialog, where you choose which folder your photos are in. Once you navigate your way to that folder, click the OK button, then go to the bottom-right corner of the iTunes window, and click the Apply button to upload the photos in that folder to your iPhone. If you have subfolders in that folder, you can also click the Selected Folders radio button, and turn on the checkboxes only for the subfolders you want to upload. The subfolders will show up as albums on your iPhone.

Viewing Your Photos

Once you've imported photos into your iPhone, to see them, start at the Home screen, then tap on the Photos button. This brings up the Photo Albums screen and at the top is your Camera Roll (the photos taken with the iPhone's built-in camera), then your Photo Library (all the photos you've imported into your iPhone all lumped together), and then a list of any separate photo albums you created, like family photos, vacation photos, etc., using Apple's iPhoto application (on a Mac), or Photoshop Album or Photoshop Elements (on a PC), or by importing them from folders. To see your photos as thumbnails, tap on any album. You can scroll through your thumbnails by swiping your finger up/down the screen. To see any photo full screen, just tap on it. Once your photo is full screen, you can see other photos in that album at that size by swiping your finger on the screen in the direction you want to scroll. If your photo bounces like it's hitting a wall, you've reached the end of that album, so swipe back in the other direction.

iTip

If a photo is wide (in landscape orientation), to see that photo as large as possible, just turn your iPhone sideways, and the photo automatically adjusts so it's viewed horizontally. To see a vertical (portrait orientation) photo as large as possible, just turn your iPhone back upright.

Viewing a Slide Show

SCOTT KELBY

To see a slide show of your photos, start at the Home screen, then tap on the Photos button to bring up the Photo Albums screen. To see any photo album as a slide show, just tap on the album, then when the thumbnails appear, at the bottom of the screen is a Play button. Tap on it to start the slide show. To stop your slide show, just tap the screen once, then tap the name of your album that appears in the top-left corner of the screen. iPhone slide shows come complete with smooth, built-in dissolve transitions between each photo, but if you want to choose a different type of dissolve, or change the length of time each photo appears onscreen, then start at the Home screen and tap on Settings. When the Settings screen appears, tap on Photos, which brings up a list of options for your slide show. To change any setting, just click on it. You can also turn on Repeat to loop your slide show, or Shuffle to play your slides in a random order. When you're done, tap the Settings button in the upper-left corner.

Pausing and Manually Viewing Slide Shows

SCOTT KELBY

To pause a running slide show, just tap the screen. This not only pauses the current slide show, but it brings up an additional set of slide show controls at the bottom of the screen. They include left and right arrow buttons to manually advance your slides, a Play button to restart your slide show, and an Options button (on the left) that brings up a pop-up menu which lets you choose the currently displayed photo as your startup wallpaper, email the photo, assign the photo to a contact, or send the photo to your MobileMe Web gallery (if you have a MobileMe account). At the top of the screen, it now displays which number photo you're currently on (for example, photo 2 of 9), and there's a button on the top left that lets you return to the thumbnail list of photos for that album.

---

iTip

If you're looking inside an album, and want to know how many photos are in it without having to return to the main Photo Albums screen, just scroll all the way to the bottom of the thumbnails and it will display how many photos are in that album.

Adding Background Music to Your Slide Show

There really isn't a slide show feature that lets you include music (at least at this point), so we're going to do a workaround (It's a little clunky, but it works). Start at the Home screen, then tap on the orange iPod button. In the iPod screen, tap on Songs and scroll to the song you want as background music for your slide show. Tap the song and the music starts playing (as long as you don't have your headset plugged in, you'll hear the music playing through your iPhone's built-in speaker). Now, press the Home button to return to the Home screen, tap on the Photos button, tap on the album you want to see as a slide show, then tap the Play button that appears at the bottom of the thumbnails screen. There you have it—your slide show playing with background music playing behind it.

iTip

To change the order of your photos, you have to go back to your computer. Change the order the photos appear in the album, then go to iTunes, sync your iPhone with your computer, and it will update your iPhone with the new order.

Using the Built-In Camera

SCOTT KELBY

To take photos with the iPhone's built-in camera, start at the Home screen and tap on Camera. This takes you to the Camera screen, and when you first get there you'll see what appears to be a closed shutter, but after just a couple of seconds, you'll see a full-color image of what you're pointing your iPhone at (the camera is on the back side of the iPhone—on the top left). To take a photo, tap the camera shutter button at the bottom center of the screen. Three things will quickly happen: (1) you'll hear a shutter sound, (2) you'll see the shutter graphic appear, like a shutter opening and closing, and (3) you'll see the photo you just took appear onscreen for about two seconds. Then it gets sucked down into the tiny icon on the bottom-left side on the screen, where it will remain until you tap on that little icon. So, tap on that little icon. This brings up the Camera Roll screen and this is where all the photos you've taken with the built-in camera are stored. To see any photo full screen, just tap on it. A set of navigation controls appears at the bottom of the screen, but disappears in a couple of seconds. To bring the controls back, just tap once on the photo.

Viewing Photos Taken with the Camera

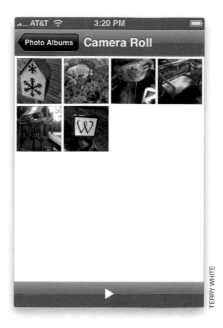

To see photos you've taken with the built-in camera, start at the Home screen and tap on the Photos button to bring up the Photo Albums screen. At the top of the screen is the Camera Roll—these are the photos taken with the built-in camera, so tap on Camera Roll. This brings up the Camera Roll screen (shown above), with thumbnails of the photos you've taken. To see a photo full-screen size, just tap on it. To delete a selected photo, tap the Trash button at the bottom-right corner of the screen. (*Note:* If you don't see the Trash button, tap once in the center of the full-screen photo and the controls will appear at the bottom of the screen again.) To see a slide show of the photos in your Camera Roll, tap the Play button at the bottom of the screen. To use a photo as a wallpaper background, email it to a friend, assign it to a contact, or send it to your MobileMe Web gallery, tap the button at the bottom-left corner and buttons for each of those tasks will appear onscreen—just tap the one you want (if you don't have a MobileMe account, you won't see this option).

Zooming In on Photos

To get a closer look at any photo, either in your photo albums or a photo you've taken with the built-in camera, just tap on the photo to see it full screen, then place your pinched fingers in the center of the screen and spread them outward to zoom in. To zoom in tighter, pinch-and-spread outward once again. To return to the normal-sized view, just double-tap on the screen.

Receiving Photos from a Cell Phone

Although the iPhone lets you email a photo to someone, it doesn't let you send a photo directly to someone else's cell phone (see Chapter 9 for a workaround tip on sending a photo to someone's cell phone). And if you want someone to send you a photo, they'll need to email it to you. However, what if someone takes a photo with their cell phone, and they send it directly to your iPhone—then what happens? Believe it or not, your iPhone gives you a message that you've received a multimedia message that cannot be read by your iPhone, and then it gives you a website where AT&T has posted the photo sent by your friend (check with your carrier if you don't have AT&T). They also give you a one-time username and password, so you can go online and see the photo that was sent. It's really a very clever workaround. Except for one thing: you have to write down the username and password, because while there is a direct link to the site in the message, there's no way to copy-and-paste the username and password. Hey, I said it was a very clever workaround—I never said it was perfect.

Making a Photo Your iPhone's Wallpaper

TERRY WHITE

When you wake your iPhone from sleep, or when you're making a call, you can have a photo appear as your background image (for example, I like to see a peaceful landscape shot every time I wake my iPhone—it just puts a smile on my face). To do this, start at the Home screen and tap on Photos. When the Photo Albums screen appears, tap on the album that contains the photo you want to use as your background wallpaper. Then, when you see the thumbnails screen appear, tap once on the photo you want to use, then tap on the button in the bottom-left corner of the screen and a list of options pops up. Tap the Use As Wallpaper button, and then a new screen appears where you can adjust the size and position of your photo by tapping-and-dragging it around on the screen and pinching out to zoom in on the photo. When it looks good to you, choose Set Wallpaper, and you're set (sorry, that was lame).

How to Email a Photo

To email a photo to someone's email account, start at the Home screen, then tap on the Photo button. If the photo you want to send is one you took with your built-in camera, tap on Camera Roll, then tap on the photo you want to email. If it's from one of your photo albums, tap on the album, then on the thumbnail of the photo you want to email. Either way, once the selected photo appears at full-screen size, tap the button on the bottom-left corner of the screen to bring up the options for what to do with that photo. Tap on Email Photo, which takes you to the New Message screen. Tap on the To field and the keyboard appears, so you can enter the email address for the person you're send-ing the photo to (if the person you're emailing is in your All Contacts list, tap on the blue circle on the right side of the To field). You can tap on the Cc/Bcc, From field to ac-tivate the other fields and send a copy to another email address, and the Subject field to enter the subject line for your email. You'll see that your photo is already included at the bottom of the email message, so once that info is entered, you can email your photo by tapping the Send button in the upper-right corner of the screen. (*Note*: See Chapter 9 for a workaround tip on sending a photo directly to another cell phone.)

Post a Photo to a MobileMe Gallery

If you have a MobileMe account and have it set up on your iPhone, you can send photos directly from your iPhone's Photo Library or Camera Roll to a MobileMe Web gallery. The first thing you'll need to do is log into your MobileMe account from your computer—point your browser to www.me.com and enter your username and password. Click the Gallery icon (it's a picture of a flower) at the top left of the page. Now add a new gallery by clicking the + (plus sign) button in the lower-left corner of the page and you'll be presented with a dialog of options. Turn on the Adding of Photos Via Email or iPhone checkbox. You can also specify whether or not you want others to be able to upload or download to this gallery via a Web browser and whether you want the gallery to be displayed on your main gallery page or not—if you choose not to display it on your gallery page, then you'll need to provide people with the URL to get to it. Once you're satisfied with the options, click Create. Now go back to your iPhone, tap Photos from the Home screen, and navigate to a photo you wish to send to your new gallery. Once it's full screen, tap the button at the bottom left, which looks like a curved arrow pointing to the right, and then tap Send to MobileMe. This will compose an email with the photo attached to the special email address for your gallery. There's no reason to add anything to the email, such as text, as no one is going to read it. Just tap the Send button and your photo will automatically be uploaded to your MobileMe gallery. Your gallery will be viewable to others by sending them to http://gallery.me.com/Your_User_Name.

Downloading Photos from Your iPhone

Although you use iTunes to manage just about everything on your iPhone, when it comes to your iPhone's built-in camera, you treat it just like you would any other digital camera. In other words, when you plug your iPhone in and it has photos on it that you've taken, whatever software you have installed to import photos will likely automatically launch. For example, if you're a Mac user, chances are iPhoto or Image Capture will launch and offer to import your shots. If you're a Windows user, the Autoplay dialog or Windows Camera Wizard will kick in. You're not limited to these apps, though. You can use Photoshop Elements, Photoshop Lightroom, Apple's Aperture, Adobe Bridge's Photo Downloader, or just about any other app that can bring images in from a camera. If you just want to download the images you've taken to a folder, then you can use Image Capture on your Mac or Autoplay on your Windows PC. Both of these apps will download the images you've taken with your iPhone to a folder of your choice on your computer. From there you can do whatever you'd like with them, as they are standard JPEG files.

Chapter Nine
Cereal Killer
Killer Tips and Tricks

 This is the second edition of this book, and anytime we get a chance to update a book, we want to do more than just update the book with the new features—we want the new book to be better than the first version, because apparently we have something terribly wrong with how our brains are wired. You see, most authors are content with just updating their books, but Terry and I look at those other authors, who have things like a family life, and friends, and free time, and successful careers outside writing, and we say to ourselves, "Look at those suckers. They're out there having fun and enjoying their families when they could be indoors, tied endlessly to their laptops, typing on a keyboard, until they have nothing but bloody stumps where their fingers used to be." We laugh and poke fun at these "fun-loving" authors because clearly, they're just not "committed" enough to risk their marriages, jobs, and the occasional felony charge to really take their books to the next level. So, when Terry came up with the idea to add this chapter, even though we had already finished all the writing and updating, and the book was due to go to press, as you might imagine, it added some stress. Now, you know and I know how harmful stress can be to your health and well-being. In fact, many unlicensed physicians now feel that anxiety from writing extra tips like this can lead to stress-related health problems—in particular, cardiovascular problems that increase your risk of strokes and heart attacks, which is precisely why we named this chapter "Cereal Killer," after the song by Method Man and Redman. We considered the name "Death Trip," but only in passing.

Master the Virtual Keyboard

When you first type on the iPhone keyboard, you'll probably want to correct your mistakes as you type, but the iPhone is intelligent and auto corrects most mistakes. It compares what you're typing to the adjacent keys and usually guesses the right word, so keep typing. If you did make a mistake that you wish to correct, you don't have to delete the whole word. Tap-and-hold over the word and a magnifying glass appears. You can now slide your finger over to move the cursor to where you want to make your change or deletion. If you start typing a word that is familiar to the iPhone, it may offer a suggestion. If the suggestion is correct, hit the space bar; if it's incorrect, keep typing. When you finish a sentence, there is no reason to hit period and then the space bar. If you double-tap the space bar, the iPhone will insert a period and a space, as well as enable the Shift key for the next sentence. Caps Lock is off by default, but you can enable it in your Keyboard settings (on the Home screen, tap on Settings, then tap on General, and then tap on Keyboard). Once it's enabled, you can double-tap the Shift key to turn Caps Lock on.

iTip

There's no way to turn off the iPhone's corrections, but there's a workaround: Type a lowercase letter or number, then move the cursor to the left of it. Now you can type and the iPhone won't correct you, because it thinks you're in the middle of a word (you'll lose the benefit of double-tapping to get a period). When you're done typing, just delete the lowercase letter or number.

Access Those Special Accent Characters

If you were wondering how to type special accent characters on your iPhone keyboard, there is a way. The next time you need to type an accent character, simply tap-and-hold on the key that would have the accent over it and the available accent characters will pop up for you to choose from. Slide your finger over to the character you want and tap it to choose it.

.org and Other Domains Are One Tap Away in Safari

Not every site that you're going to want to surf ends in .com, but luckily, you can use the .com button to access the rest of the most commonly used top-level domains on the Internet. Once you're in the Safari app and you've keyed in the beginning of the URL you want, if you want to use an alternate domain ending (such as .org), tap-and-hold on the .com button and once the choices pop up, slide your finger over them and choose the one you want.

The Secret .com Button in Mail

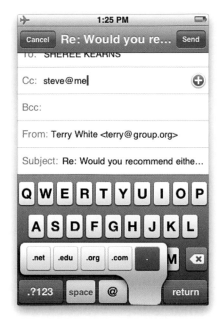

Did you ever notice how there's a .com button in the Safari app's keyboard, but there isn't one in the Mail app? Actually there is one, it's just not obvious. The next time you want to end an email address that you're typing with .com, .org, etc., just tap-and-hold on the period button until the choices pop up. Then slide your finger over and choose the domain ending that you wish to use. Actually, you can use this feature whenever you are using a keyboard with a period key. I've used this feature in third-party apps, as well.

Switch Keyboards for Your Language

The iPhone is available in several countries now and therefore has to support different languages and different keyboard layouts. You can actually enable multiple foreign language keyboards and switch between them, as needed. Before you can switch keyboards, you must first turn on the keyboards you'll want to use. To do this, tap Settings from the Home screen, then tap General, and from there tap International, and then tap Keyboards. This screen will list all the various keyboard languages that you can enable. Turn on the keyboard(s) that you want, and now when you're in an app that requires you to key something in, you'll see a little globe button on the bottom left of the keyboard. Just tap that button to switch between the keyboards you've enabled.

---

iTip

A friend of mine speaks Spanish and has an iPhone. He says that he sometimes types emails in English and sometimes in Spanish. So, of course, if he's typing in Spanish, the iPhone tries to correct him in the wrong language. Luckily, as I said above, the iPhone now supports multiple language keyboards. Now, he simply enables the Spanish keyboard (following the method described above), which puts the little globe button on the bottom left of the keyboard, so that while he's typing, he can tap it to switch between languages. This way, he can mix English and Spanish in the same email.

Control the Size of Your Caller ID Photos

If you've added photos to your contacts, you may have noticed that some of them display full screen and some only display in the upper-right corner of the screen when a contact calls you. How can you control this? It all boils down to how the photo was added to the contact. If you added the photo to your contact from your computer's address book (Address Book on the Mac or Outlook on the PC), then it will likely display the photo small in the upper-right corner of the screen. However, if you added the photo to your contact directly on the iPhone, either using the iPhone's camera or from photos in your iPhone's Photo Library, they will display full screen when the contact calls.

---

iTip

You may have noticed, in the example above on the left, it says "Carla or Terry White home." This is because I have two contacts in my iPhone with the same home number. The iPhone doesn't choose sides—it just displays both names when a call comes in from that number.

Get to Your Phone Favorites or iPod Controls Quickly

By default, double-clicking the Home button will automatically take you to your Phone app Favorites, but you can configure the Home button to take you to either the Home screen or the iPod app, as well. Also, by default, if you are using the iPod app, double-clicking the Home button will bring up the iPod controls, so that you can advance to the next song, pause, go back to the beginning of the track, go to the previous track, or adjust the volume. To change your Home button preference or to turn off the iPod controls, tap on Settings from the Home screen and then tap General. Scroll down and tap Home Button for these preferences.

Apple's iPhone Bluetooth Headset

Apple makes a very cool Bluetooth headset for the iPhone. It's smaller than most and is very comfortable to wear in your ear. Also, unlike most Bluetooth headsets, there is no gaudy flashing light on the side of your head while you're wearing it. If you use the Apple iPhone Bluetooth Headset, its battery status will display in the top-right corner of the iPhone's screen. You'll see the battery status while the iPhone and headset are in use and while the iPhone and headset are charging via the supplied cable or cradle.

Tips for the International Traveler

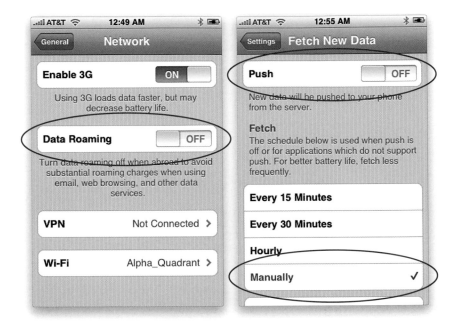

While you might have an unlimited data plan at a set price with your carrier, all bets are off when you travel outside your country. Data roaming charges can be astronomical for simple things like checking your email. You could be getting charged for every kilobit that comes in and goes out. Luckily, there are some ways to make sure you don't come home to a bill the size of a mortgage payment. First, you have to decide if you want to be able to make calls while you travel. If so, you may need to contact your carrier and make sure that international calling is enabled on your account. The next thing you want to make sure of is that you aren't roaming on a data network. To prevent this from happening, make sure your Data Roaming is set to OFF (tap on Settings on the Home Screen, then tap General, and then tap Network). Of course, this means that you won't be able to surf the Web, check email, etc., while you're out and about. However, you will still be able to connect to Wi-Fi networks. Let's say that you are willing to pay for data roaming, then you can turn Data Roaming on, but I recommend that you turn off Push (on the Settings screen, tap Fetch New Data), so that your iPhone isn't constantly keeping in touch with your email server. Also, change the Fetch interval to Manually. This way, you'll only be using data when you manually check for email, or surf the Web, or run Web-based apps.

Create Your Own Ringtones with GarageBand

If you want your iPhone to ring with your own tunes or sounds, you can make your own ringtones using Apple's GarageBand (4.1.2 or higher). GarageBand is included with iLife '08 and ships on all new Macs. To make a custom ringtone in GarageBand, launch the GarageBand app found in your Applications folder, then create a new song. Now you can either mix your own track using the software instruments, real instruments (if you're musically inclined), software loops, or vocals from your built-in or external microphone. If you're not musically inclined, you can import one of the many supported sound file formats, such as MP3. Trim your song or composition to be no longer than 30 seconds and make sure it's set to loop. Once you have built the perfect ringtone, choose Send Ringtone to iTunes from the Share menu. Your custom ringtone will be created and appear as an available ringtone in your iTunes Ringtones Library. You can then sync it and use it on your iPhone.

Create Your Own Ringtones with iTunes

While it's great to buy ringtones from the iTunes Store, you may want to make a ringtone from a sound file or song that isn't available in the iTunes Store—maybe one of your kids singing or a song from a CD. You can create a ringtone from a non-iTunes purchased song using iTunes, but there are a few steps involved: First, in your iTunes preferences, make sure your iTunes Import Using preference is set to AAC Encoder (choose Preferences from the iTunes [PC: Edit] menu, click the General icon, then click the Import Settings button). Import your song into iTunes (MP3s and AAC files work great). Find the 30 seconds (or less) of the song that you want by playing the song and noting the segment start and end times in the progress bar at the top of the iTunes window. Choose Get Info from the File menu, click on the Options tab, enter the Start Time and Stop Time for your 30-second ringtone, and click OK. Choose Create AAC Version from the Advanced menu and this will create a 30-second version of the song, right beneath the original. Control-click (PC: Right-click) on it and choose Show in Finder (PC: Show in Explorer). When the file appears, duplicate it and change the copy's extension from .m4a to .m4r, and then go back to iTunes and delete the 30-second version you created earlier. Now go back to the Finder window and drag the new .m4r version of your file onto the iTunes icon in your Dock (PC: Taskbar) to import your new ringtone into your Ringtones Library. When you connect your iPhone to iTunes, your new ringtone will be available to sync. Don't forget to go back and turn off the Start Time and Stop Time checkboxes for your original song, so that it will play in its entirety again.

Use the Contacts App While on a Call

You might be asking yourself, "Why is there a separate Contacts app?" which, by default, appears on your second Home screen. After all, you have complete access to your contacts in the Phone app. There are two reasons for the separate Contacts app: The first is to simply make it easier to get to your contacts when you don't want to make a call. Sometimes you may just want to look up an address or some other information on a contact without having to first tap Phone and then tap the Contacts button in the Phone app. The second has to do with managing your contacts while on a call. When you have a call in progress, you can access your contacts directly by tapping the Contacts button on the call screen, however, you'll be in a view-only mode. Just the other day, I was on a call with someone and they wanted to give me their new mobile number, and I wanted to enter that number directly into their Contacts record. By accessing the Home screen and then tapping the separate Contacts app, I was able to edit that contact's information while talking with them using the Speaker option.

Dial Another Number for a Favorite Contact

The Favorites screen in the Phone app of the iPhone is great because you can just tap the name of the contact you wish to dial and the iPhone immediately begins calling that contact. However, sometimes the contact may have multiple phone numbers, such as home, work, mobile, etc., and you may not wish to put every number in as a Favorite. So, the next time you need to dial a number for a Favorite contact that's not actually saved as a Favorite, bring up your Favorites list from the Phone app and then tap the blue arrow button next to the Favorite contact's name. This will take you to their Info screen and show you all the additional numbers you have for that contact. From there, you can dial one of their other numbers to reach them.

Where Is That Call Coming From?

The next time you get a call from an unfamiliar area code and number, you can actually see where that call came from. The call will appear in the Recents screen of the Phone app, and once you see the number in the list, just tap the blue arrow button to the right of the number. You'll be taken to the screen shown above, which not only lists the number, but also the city and state that the call originated from, as well as the time and date.

Jump to the Search Bar or Top of Any Page

There's a nice search feature in the Contacts app. However, it's only available at the top of the Contacts screen. If you've scrolled down several contacts, it can be a pain having to scroll up just to key in a search, but here's a super-fast way to get there: just tap right on the top bar (I usually tap on the time right in the middle of the top bar), and that will scroll you back up to the top instantly. This works in Safari, if you've scrolled down on a webpage, and other apps, as well.

Where Does That Link Actually Go?

One of the features I really like about Apple's desktop Mail application is the ability to hover my cursor over a Web address in an email to see where that address really goes. Spammers and phishing scams often use hidden URLs under what looks to be a legitimate address. There's a way to do this on your iPhone, as well. Bring up the email with the questionable Web link in it, and simply tap-and-hold on the link for a few seconds, and the actual URL to where the link will take you will pop up. This also works in Safari with links on webpages.

Use the Next Button When Filling Out a Form

The next time you're filling out a form on a webpage in Safari, you might want to try the built-in field navigation buttons. Using the Previous and Next buttons are a lot easier, at times, than having to manually scroll and tap on the next field. After you make your selection in a pop-up menu, or key in the information in a text field, just tap the Next button and Safari will automatically advance to the next field on the form, even if it has to scroll the webpage to do so. Just tap the Previous button to go back to a field.

Save an Image from a Webpage

If you've ever surfed to a webpage that had an image on it that you wanted to keep, you can save the Image directly from the webpage to your iPhone's Camera Roll. Once the shot is in your Camera Roll, you can email it, sync it to your computer, use it as your wallpaper, or assign it to a contact. To save an image from a webpage to your Camera Roll, navigate to the webpage that has the picture on it using the Safari app. Then, tap-and-hold on the picture and a menu will pop up with the option to save the image. Once you tap Save Image, the menu will go away and the image will be in your Camera Roll. Access the image in your Camera Roll by tapping Photos from the Home screen.

Mobile Versions of Your Favorite Sites

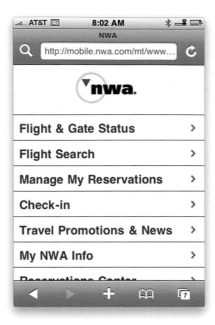

It's great that the iPhone has a Web browser to display websites in all their glory. However, let's face it, many websites have unnecessary fluff and clutter—such as ads and large graphics—that take time to load, even on a 3G network. In many cases, these websites have a "mobile" version or even a version specifically formatted for the iPhone/iPod touch. This makes getting to the information you want *much* faster! Living in the Midwest, I fly on Northwest Airlines quite a bit. Although the nwa.com site loads just fine on the iPhone, the mobile.nwa.com site loads much faster, and is now formatted for the iPhone. When I'm just trying to see if my flight is on time, I really don't need to see all the other things on the site, such as the "deals" section, I just need the info about my flight. The mobile version of this site rocks! Check your favorite site to see if they have a bandwidth-conscious mobile version. Oftentimes, it's as simple as typing "mobile" or "m" in front of the domain name, such as mobile.fandango.com or m.usatoday.com. You may be surprised to see that they even have one that's formatted just for the iPhone.

Find an Airport in the Maps App Quickly

Quick, what's the address of the airport? Exactly! Does anyone really know? You don't really have to know the address, because the Maps app has got you covered. All you need to know is the airport code. For example, if you were trying to get to Chicago O'Hare International Airport, simply tap on the Maps app and type ORD into the search field, or you'd type SFO if you were trying to get to San Francisco International Airport. Or if you were trying to get to my airport, it would be DTW (for Detroit Metropolitan Wayne County Airport). Tap the Search button and the Maps app will zero right in on the airport's location. From there, you can plot your route.

Search for Contacts in Maps

Now that the iPhone has a search feature in the Contacts app, you can search for your contacts in the Maps app if you have their address information. Let's say that you want to map a route to one of your contacts and call them before you head out. Well, you can do it all from the Maps app. Tap the Maps button on the Home screen, and when you start typing in your contact's name in the search field, the Maps app automatically starts searching through your contacts. Once you find the contact you want, just tap on it and Maps will locate that contact on the map. If you want to call that contact, just tap the blue arrow button to the right of the pin, and you'll be taken to the contact's Info screen, which has the phone number. You can then just tap the phone number to dial it.

Build Up Your Contacts from the Maps App

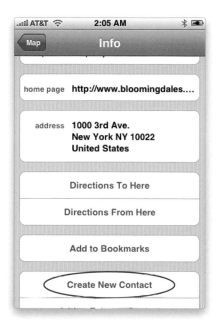

The built-in Google Maps app is a wonderful source for new contacts. That's right, if you look up a business by doing a search in the Maps app, and it's a business that you plan to continue to visit or call, why not add it to your Contacts list? But don't type it in manually, let the Maps app create the new contact for you, complete with phone number, address, and even the website. Tap the Maps button on the Home screen and then do a search for the business you'd like to add to your Contacts list. Once you find the one you want, tap the blue arrow button to the right of the pin. On the new Info screen that appears, scroll down and you'll see a Create New Contact button. Tap Create New Contact, then tap Save, and this information will automatically be added to your Contacts list.

Get Notes from Your Computer on Your iPhone

Currently, notes created on your iPhone aren't synced to your computer (they are backed up, though). However, I do have a workaround for creating notes on your computer and having them sync to the iPhone. This tip will require that you have at least one email account that is IMAP-based, such as MobileMe, Gmail, or Microsoft Exchange. With an IMAP-based email account, you can create folders that reside on a server and, therefore, show up on the iPhone. So, first you'll need to create a new folder/mailbox in your email client and make sure the location is on the server. If you are a Mac user running OS X v10.5 Leopard or higher, the Mail app has a Notes feature, where you can compose a note and then drag it to your newly created folder. Once it's in that folder, it will automatically be uploaded to the mail server and become available on your iPhone. In my example here, I created a Notes folder on my MobileMe email account server and, as you can see here on the right, that folder is also available on my iPhone. If you're on a Windows PC or are running OS X v10.4 Tiger on a Mac, you can simply create an email containing the note and email it to the account you created the Notes folder in, then just drag the email into the Notes folder and it will be available on your iPhone. If you really want to create notes on the iPhone and get them back to your computer, you can use the iPhone's Notes app to create your note, then email the note to yourself from your iPhone and move it to your Notes folder. It will now be available both on your iPhone and your computer. Lastly, if you create a dummy contact, you can use the Note field of that contact to sync notes back and forth between your iPhone and computer.

The iPhone at Work: Enterprise Support

If your company uses Microsoft Exchange for their email, calendar, and contact serving needs, or uses Cisco VPN, you're in luck! The iPhone supports Microsoft's Active Sync and certain Cisco VPN routers for secure connections outside the firewall (currently, not all Cisco VPN routers support iPhone VPN capabilities). Depending on your IT department, they may be able to give you the settings to key in for your Exchange account or your VPN setup, or they may have web-based profiles that will automatically configure the iPhone for you to access your work email and other services. My company's IT department gave me a URL that basically set up my iPhone automatically with profiles that enforce company policies, such as requiring a passcode to access the phone after so many minutes of inactivity. Also, if my iPhone is ever lost or stolen, I can contact our support desk and they can remotely wipe the iPhone over the air. Once the wipe process starts, nothing can stop it—not even powering it down or removing the SIM card. As soon as the iPhone is powered back on, the wipe will continue. If you configure the iPhone to receive your contacts via Exchange, you'll also get access to your company's LDAP directory that you can search right on the iPhone. It's impossible to cover every thinkable corporate setup here, so my thought was to simply arm you with the information you need to go back to your IT folks and request the setup info for your iPhone. Also note that since the iPhone supports Cisco VPN, you'll be able to access things like webpages on your company's intranet from your iPhone.

Work and Play

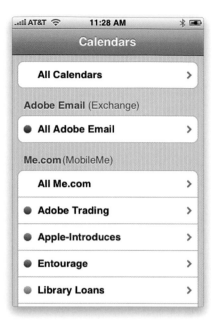

The iPhone has always supported multiple email accounts, so having your personal email and work email on the iPhone wasn't a problem. However, now that the iPhone supports Microsoft Exchange corporate email and "pushed" email from Apple's MobileMe service, things are a bit more complicated. For starters, you can only have one Exchange account set up at a time. This probably isn't a big deal for you, because you probably only have one email account that uses Exchange, but here's the kicker: if you use your work calendar via Exchange, then you won't be able to sync personal calendars via iCal or Outlook through iTunes. All is not lost though, as you can use MobileMe to push your personal calendars to the iPhone. So basically, you'll have your work calendar via Exchange and your personal calendars through MobileMe, and you can switch between them to view appointments on the iPhone.

Use Contact and Calendar Notes

Did you ever go to check in at a hotel, only to have the clerk tell you that they can't find your reservation? They ask you for your confirmation number and then you have to start digging, or maybe they don't have your Frequent Stay/Flyer number on file and you, again, have to find it. Why not have these little important pieces of information in the Note field of a contact or in the Notes field of your calendar event? For example, when I'm going to take a flight somewhere, I usually block that time out on my calendar. I also put the address of the hotel and my confirmation number right in the Notes field of this event. This way, when I get to the front desk of the hotel or when I get in the back of the taxi, I'm just a couple of taps away from the information that I need. You can add these little notes either on your computer's calendar that you have syncing/pushing to your iPhone or directly on the iPhone's calendar itself. Just tap Edit in the Calendar's Event screen, and then tap the Notes button at the bottom. Type in any information you'll need once you get to your destination and, once you save the info, you'll be able to see it by tapping the event in your calendar.

Test Your Speed on the Go (Is 3G Really Fast?)

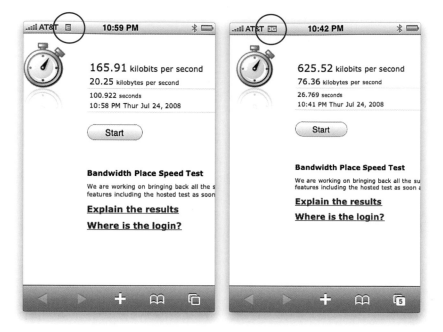

If you have an iPhone 3G, you're probably wondering if it really is faster than EDGE networks. One way to find out is to run a speed test while you're connected to a 3G network. The website that I use is www.bandwidthplace.com, however, I can never remember the name of the website, so I have it bookmarked in my iPhone Bookmarks in an iPhone folder. This way, if I ever decide to test my speed on the fly, the site is a couple of taps away. You can even make it a Web clip on your Home screen to have one-tap access to it. You can find the speed test on the website under the Resources link at the top of the page.

Videos: Full Screen or 16:9

If you're watching a widescreen video, there's a good chance that the video has a 16:9 aspect ratio. However, the iPhone's screen isn't truly 16:9, so you would get letterboxing (black bars at the top and bottom of the movie). The iPhone does, though, default to playing your movie and filling up the screen, but the only way to accomplish this is to crop off the left and right edges of the movie. So, if you want to see the full movie (letter-boxed), just double tap on it while it's playing and you can toggle between full screen and true 16:9.

Play Videos Back to Back

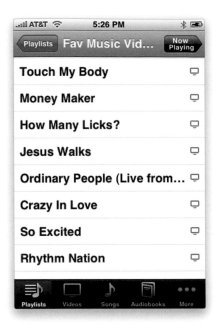

When you add music videos to your iPhone, they show up in the Videos screen of the iPod app. However, if you play one from there, it stops at the end and does not advance to the next one. So, if you want your videos to play back to back, put them in a playlist in iTunes. That's right! We typically think of playlists for our music, however, the iPhone will allow you to play videos that are in a playlist by accessing your playlists feature on your iPod app (tap the iPod button on your Home screen, then tap the Playlists button). Once you play the first video, the next one will automatically start playing after the first one is done.

---

iTip

If you enable syncing of music videos in iTunes by turning on the Include Music Videos checkbox in the Music preferences, it will sync all of your music videos if you're syncing your entire Music Library. If you don't wish to carry all of your music videos on your iPhone, then just sync selected playlists instead, and put your favorite music videos in a playlist that will be synced to your iPhone.

Take Your Own Movies with You

Although you can buy and rent movies from the iTunes Store, chances are you also have your own movie collection—home movies that you've created or movies you've purchased on DVD. Although iTunes does let you convert your music CDs into iPhone- and iPod-compatible formats, it doesn't convert regular movie DVDs that you purchased, but there's a workaround. Now, before I go on any further, you'll have to check the laws in your country and the license agreements of the DVDs you've purchased to make sure that you are not breaking any laws by converting them for your own personal use on another device, such as the iPhone. Okay, now that I've cleared the air on that, let's talk about various conversion methods. If you have a movie that you've created and it's in QuickTime format, you can import that movie into iTunes (by choosing Import from the File menu) and have iTunes convert it into a compatible iPhone format (by choosing Create iPod or iPhone version from the Advanced menu). But, if you have a purchased movie DVD, then you're going to need an additional application to do the conversion. My favorite app for doing these conversions is called Handbrake. It's cross-platform and, best of all, it's free! Remember, this app and this process is for your *own* personal use. It is for movies that you've created or purchased. It also works for movies you've created yourself and burned to DVD. For example, the movie shown above was one of my own home movies of a lecture that I burned to DVD. Then I decided that I wanted a copy on my iPhone. So, I imported it into iTunes, converted it, and then synced it to my iPhone.

Movie DVDs That Contain a Digital Copy

Another trend that I'm starting to see is some movie studios now sell DVDs that include a digital copy. That's right, these DVDs include a second disc that is already formatted for your iPhone or iPod. It's the best of both worlds. You get a DVD or Blu-ray disc to watch on your big-screen TV, and you get a second disc that you put into your computer. Once you authorize the digital copy to your iTunes account, it's automatically copied into iTunes and therefore available to sync to your iPhone. The next time you're buying a movie on DVD or Blu-ray, be sure to check the packaging to see if it includes a digital copy.

TiVo To Go

If you own a TiVo Series 2, Series 3, or TiVo HD, then you have the ability to transfer most recorded content from your TiVo to your computer using TiVo's TiVo-To-Go option. On a PC, there is a TiVo-To-Go app that you can download directly from TiVo's website (TiVo Desktop Plus software for PC). On a Mac, this functionality is available through Roxio's Toast Titanium software CD/DVD burning app. Once you have the TiVo-To-Go option configured, you can then transfer unrestricted content directly from your TiVo DVR to your Mac or PC over your home network. When the content has been transferred to your computer, you can then use the TiVo or Toast software to convert it to a format that will play on your iPhone. Depending on the size of the show (standard def vs. HD), it could take several minutes or hours to transfer the content and convert it, so plan ahead.

Transferring Your Old iPhone to a New User

I'm on my third iPhone now. I went from the original 8-GB iPhone to the 16-GB iPhone and now to the iPhone 3G. Each time I upgraded, I either passed on my older model to a family member or sold it. So how does the recipient of your old iPhone get up and running? Actually, the process is easier than you think. When you get your new iPhone, your carrier will transfer your old number and account to it. Therefore your old iPhone is still accessible, but won't have any service, so you could use it as an iPod touch. If you want to transfer it to someone else, first go into the Settings from the Home screen, then tap General, and scroll down and tap Reset. When you tap Reset, there will be a choice to Erase All Content and Settings. This will erase all of your information off the old phone. You can also do this in iTunes by connecting your old iPhone to your computer, clicking on the Summary tab in the iPhone preferences, and then clicking on Restore in the Version section (but the Reset option on the iPhone actually does a more secure wipe of the iPhone). Now that the old iPhone is clear of your info, when you give or sell it to the next person, all they have to do is connect it to their computer and activate it in iTunes. They can set up a new account right then and there. *Note:* Depending on how you upgraded to your new iPhone, the person you're handing the old one down to may need a new SIM card, and they can go to their iPhone carrier to pick one up, if necessary.

Unused Applications on Your Home Screen

The iPhone has some very useful apps built in. However, you may not need every app that's there. For example, if you don't play the stock market, then you might not need the Stocks app. Or maybe you don't watch a lot of YouTube videos. Although you can't delete these apps from the iPhone (the apps that come built in), you can move them off your main Home screen, and you can have up to nine Home screens. So, this means that you can move less frequently used apps to another screen. To do this, tap-and-hold on any app for a few seconds until all the icons start to wiggle. Now simply tap-and-drag the icon of the app you no longer want on your main Home screen to the right edge of the screen. This will switch the iPhone to the next Home screen. You can either release the icon there or drag it to the right edge again to advance to the third screen, and so on. Once you get to the screen that you want to put this app on, just release it there. When you have moved all of the apps off the main Home screen that you no longer want to see there, just click the Home button to stop the icons from wiggling and lock in your changes.

Swap Out the Apps in Your Dock

The defaullt Dock app icons   My custom Dock app icons

Although I've mentioned rearranging your apps on your various Home screens a few times now, I've run into people that don't realize that you can also move the app icons that are in the Dock. The Dock is at the bottom of each Home screen and, therefore, the apps located in it are available no matter which Home screen you happen to be looking at. Apple placed the ones there that they thought you would want to have available at all times. For example, the Phone app is there and that makes sense. After all, the iPhone is a phone. So, you should be able to access the phone functions no matter where you happen to be. However, I like to see my calendars there, so I replaced the iPod app with the Calendar app. This way, no matter which Home screen I'm on, I can not only access my calendars, but I can also see the current date. To replace a Dock app with one that you want to have there, tap-and-hold on any app for a few seconds until they all start to wiggle. Now move the app off the Dock that you don't want there anymore. This will leave room for the app that you want to put there. Just tap-and-drag the app that you want to be there down to the Dock.

Keep Your Home Screen Full

Since you can rearrange the icons on your Home screen, you probably have the first screen loaded with the apps and Web clips that you use the most. Every time you add a new app, update an existing app, or add a new Web clip, it will go to the first available spot. So if you want to keep your first Home screen (out of the nine possible Home screens that you can set up) organized just the way you want it, then fill it up so that all new apps and Web clips are forced to a subsequent screen. There is one advantage, though, to keeping space available at the bottom of each screen: it gives you a place to swipe (to go to the next screen) without accidentally launching an app.

Restore Your Home Screen Default Layout

While it's easy to get carried away rearranging your apps and Web clips from Home screen to Home screen, there may be a time that you wish to restore the main Home screen back to its original layout. Well, that's very easy to do without having to remember what the layout used to look like. Just tap the Settings button on the Home screen, then tap General, and then tap Reset. On the Reset screen, you'll see Reset Home Screen Layout. Tap that button and then tap Reset Home Screen, and you'll be back to your default layout.

Take Your Documents with You

You can sync your contacts, calendars, photos, movies, music, etc., between your computer and iPhone, but there really isn't a provision yet to sync your Documents folder on your computer. However, that doesn't mean that you can't take your documents with you. Remember the iPhone can view all kinds of email attachments, such as photos in JPEG format, PDFs, Word, Excel, and PowerPoint documents, as well as Keynote, Pages, and Numbers documents. There's nothing that says these documents have to be sent to you from other people. Let's say you have a PDF that you want to have with you when you travel. Maybe it's your itinerary, or a special map of where you're going. Simply email yourself the document you want to have with you as an email attachment. Once you receive this email on your iPhone, you can file it in a folder for quick access on the go.

Is That Email Important?

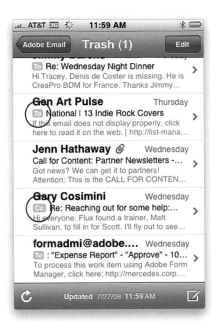

We all get bombarded with email these days. However, not all of these emails are important. One quick measure of importance is whether or not you're in the To field vs. the CC field. If someone sent a message directly to you, chances are it's probably more important than an email that you were just copied on. The iPhone's Mail app allows you to see if you are in the To field or in the CC field at a glance. However, you'll have to turn it on in the Mail settings. Tap the Settings button on the Home screen, then tap Mail, Contacts, Calendars. Be sure that Show To/CC Label is on (it is by default) and this will automatically display a "To" or "Cc" in front of each message that you are in the To or CC field of.

Send Mail from a Backup Server

If you have more than one email account, then chances are you have multiple SMTP (outgoing) email servers to choose from. Depending on the ISP (Internet service provider), you may be able to configure a backup or secondary email server to send mail from when you're on the go. For example, when I'm at home or on the road, I typically send mail from my Comcast email server. However, if for whatever reason their server is down, then I want the ability to send mail through either my yahoo.com server or my MobileMe server. You can configure your backup email server by accessing your email settings. First, tap Settings on the Home screen, then tap Mail, Contacts, Calendars on the Settings screen. Next, tap the email account that you wish to configure with a backup SMTP server, scroll down to SMTP, and tap it. You'll then be presented with a list of additional servers that you can choose from to turn on as your backup server. Just tap on Off to the right of the SMTP that you want as your backup and then tap OFF next to Server at the top to turn it on.

Manage Music Manually

Although the iPhone automatically syncs your music, movies, TV shows, etc., directly with iTunes each time you plug it in (if you have this preference set), there may be times that you just want to manually drag songs and videos over to it. Maybe you're in a situation where you have music on more than one computer, such as a laptop and a desktop. Well, you can enable the Manually Manage Music and Videos option in iTunes. Just connect your iPhone to your Mac or PC using the supplied USB cable. Once iTunes is open, you'll find this option right on the Summary screen, when your iPhone is selected in the Source list. Just turn on its checkbox.

Another Great List of iPhone Apps

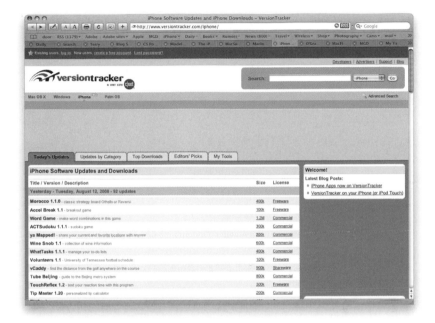

You can always see which apps are available for your iPhone by visiting the App Store on your iPhone or via the iTunes Store in iTunes on your computer. However, I've found that I like to keep track of the newest additions to the App Store, as well as the latest updates. The great folks over at versiontracker.com have now created an iPhone section on their already great site for tracking regular computer software updates. This iPhone section lists the apps on the App Store in chronological order and clicking the download links will take you right to iTunes and the App Store, so that you can complete the download or transaction.

On a Flight with Wi–Fi Access?

More and more airlines are starting to offer in-flight Internet access via Wi-Fi. While you're in the air, you're supposed to have your iPhone either off or in Airplane mode. Airplane mode allows you to continue to access your iPhone's non-wireless features, such as your iPod, games, and other third-party apps. However, if you're on a flight that offers Wi-Fi, and you want to use your iPhone's data features while still maintaining FAA safety guidelines, you can turn Wi-Fi back on. Place your iPhone in Airplane mode for takeoff and landing by going to Settings from your Home screen and then tapping OFF to the right of Airplane Mode at the top of the screen. Then once you're in the air and you're allowed to use portable electronics, go back to the same Settings screen and tap Wi-Fi, then tap the available Wi-Fi network to turn it back on and connect to the in-flight wireless.

Create a Wallpaper Business Card

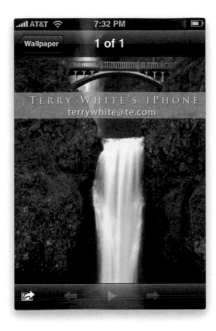

If you lose your iPhone, you may never get it back again. However, what if the person who found it was honest and wanted to return it to you? How would they know whom it belonged to? If you're like me, you'll have a passcode lock on your iPhone, so that if it is lost, no one can just pick it up and start using it. Since they can't get into it, they have no way of seeing anything on it, like your contacts, photos, etc. So unless you stick a big ugly label on the outside of the iPhone or your case, they have no way of knowing whom to return it to. Well, I've got a little bit more elegant solution than a big sticker—create (in a desktop application like Photoshop) or take a custom wallpaper image that displays your name and contact info, and then sync the image to your iPhone. Once it's there, tap Photos from the Home screen, then tap on the image in your Photo Library. Next, tap the button with the arrow at the bottom left of the screen, and then tap Use As Wallpaper from the options that appear. This way, they can call your office or home or email you that they've found your iPhone. When you turn on an iPhone, even if it's locked with a passcode, it still displays a portion of the wallpaper. By the way, it probably won't do you much good to put your iPhone number on this custom wallpaper. If you lose your iPhone and someone finds it and dials that number, they'll just be calling the phone that's in their hands. You knew this, but I had to say it.

Create an ICE Wallpaper Image

Creating a custom wallpaper image is also a good way to have an ICE (In Case of Emergency) contact display on your iPhone. Just put the ICE info of who should be called in case of emergency, and any other important information (such as medical conditions or allergies), right on your wallpaper image (the same way I suggested adding your own contact info to your wallpaper image on the previous page). Even if your iPhone is secured with a PIN, the information will still be displayed (you can still see a portion of the wallpaper when your iPhone is locked), so if something happens to you, rescue and medical personnel will know whom to contact.

 iTip

There is a third-party app called Close Call that is available for free from the App Store. This app will allow you to build a custom ICE wallpaper image from one of your existing pictures right on your iPhone. It's what I used for the wallpaper you see in the iPhone capture above.

Take a Screenshot

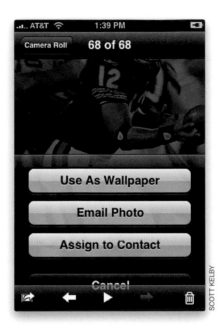

If you want to take a picture (screenshot) of something on your iPhone, there's now a built-in way to do it. Just press-and-hold the Home button and then press the Sleep/Wake button at the top right of the iPhone. The screen will flash white for a second (simulating a camera flash), and whatever was on your screen at the time will be saved to your Camera Roll as a PNG file. You can then email that file to someone or sync/download it to your computer the next time you connect your iPhone cable and sync (if you have this preference set).

iPhone Tips for Photographers

If you're a professional photographer or serious hobbyist, you've probably already figured out that the iPhone makes for a great tool to show off your shots. However, there are some other ways you can use the iPhone to help you with your future shoots. First of all, don't forget that the iPhone can have multiple albums. So this will allow you to have multiple portfolios on hand to show friends, family, and prospective clients. You can also use the iPhone to display different lighting setups that you shot, as well as shots you'd like to do. I have an "Inspiration" album on my iPhone that contains shots/ideas that I would like to do or recreate. You might also consider an album of various poses. This way you could walk right over to your model and show them exactly how you'd like them to pose without them having to leave the set and walk over to your computer. The possibilities are endless. Just sync these albums from your computer to your iPhone the next time you connect them.

Send a Photo Directly to Another Cell Phone

As of the writing of this book, the iPhone doesn't support MMS (Multimedia Messaging). Therefore, there is no direct way to send a picture that you've taken with your iPhone to another phone unless you use email. However, many people don't have email configured on their cell phones. That's why this tip will come in handy. You can send a photo directly to another phone using email and it will be received by the recipient as an MMS message. All you have to do is go to the picture you want to send either in your Photo Library or on your Camera Roll, tap on it, then tap on the arrow button at the bottom left of the screen, and choose Email Photo from the options that appear. This will insert your picture in to a new email message, where you can address your message using 1, the area code, the phone number, and the domain of the service that your recipient is using. Here are the domains for most carriers (*Note:* It's not necessary to include the dashes in between the 1, area code, and number.):

Alltel: 1-area code-number@message.alltel.com

AT&T: 1-area code-number@mms.att.net

Boost Mobile: 1-area code-number@myboostmobile.com

Cingular (AT&T): 1-area code-number@mms.mycingular.com

Einstein PCS: 1-area code-number@einstein-mms.com

Sprint: 1-area code-number@messaging.sprintpcs.com

T-Mobile: 1-area code-number@tmo-mail.net

U.S. Cellular: 1-area code-number@mms.uscc.net

Verizon Wireless: 1-area code-number@vzwpix.com

Virgin Mobile: 1-area code-number@vmobl.com

Your Photos Are Geotagged

Now when you take photos with your iPhone's built-in camera, the iPhone can use your current location and input the longitude and latitude of where you took the shot right into the photo's metadata. Some apps can actually show you on Google Maps where you were when you took the photo. Keep in mind that this location data is not 100% accurate. You could easily be off by 20–30' or more, if your iPhone doesn't have a built-in GPS (GPS is only available on iPhone 3G) or it wasn't available when you took the photo. However, you will be in the general vicinity. There are a couple of easy ways to see this data. If you're on a Mac running Mac OS X v10.5 Leopard or later, Apple's Preview app can use this metadata to show you where the shot was taken on Google Maps. Just download the photo to your Mac and then open it in Preview. Choose Inspector from the Tools menu, and then click the More Info Inspector tab in the top center of the window. There will be a Locate button at the bottom. Click the Locate button, and Preview will launch your Web browser and take you to that spot on Google Maps. If you're on a PC, you can download a free trial of Adobe's Photoshop Lightroom. Once you import your shots into Lightroom, in the Library module, scroll down in the Metadata panel (in the right side Panels area) until you see GPS under the EXIF camera data. Click the little arrow next to the longitude and latitude, and it will launch your Web browser and take you to the location on Google Maps. Also, if you upload your photos to Flickr.com, you can enable geotagging on your account in the preferences, and once it's enabled, photos from your iPhone will automatically appear on the map for your Flickr account.

Chapter Ten

The Trouble with Boys

Troubleshooting Your iPhone

 Terry asked me to write this chapter intro for two reasons: (1) it's my job to write the chapter intros, and (2) I'm not really qualified to write anything in a troubleshooting chapter. It's only because nothing has gone the slightest bit wrong with my iPhone since I bought it, so I've never had an occasion to trouble-shoot a problem. On the other hand, Terry (being a renown gadget guru and committed iPhone freak) is very hard on technology. It's not unusual to stop at Terry's house and find him taking some new gadget (like an iPhone) and exposing it to harsher conditions than your average user is likely to experience (unless he or she were to lead an expedition to Antarctica, or do so many bad things that they wind up in "the really hot place" where really bad people go—you know where I'm talking about: Phoenix). Anyway, Terry asked me to write this intro, and I have to tell you, I'm honored to do it. In fact, I'm honored to be sharing the pages of this book with him, because even though many people don't know this, Terry is the reigning Midwest freestyle clogging champion (in the men's 35–45 age bracket), and he competes nationwide at clogging conventions, state fairs, and competitions, including Clogapalooza 2008 where he took third place in the men's individual freestyle competition. I was there cheering Terry on, and I've got to tell you—he was robbed. One of the judges worked for Microsoft and, not coincidentally, was the only one to score Terry's performance as an 8.2 (all the other judges scored him as a 10). What a shame—we really thought it was "his year."

Can't Connect to Your Wi–Fi Network

Networks requiring a password may sometimes not work on the iPhone. If the network is secured by Wired Equivalent Privacy (WEP), you might want to try entering the HEX key instead of the ASCII password. To do this, you first need to locate the HEX key for your network. If it's an Apple AirPort Base Station, you can find it using the Apple AirPort Utility or AirPort Admin Utility and log into your base station. It's called Equivalent Network Password under the Base Station menu. If you have a third-party wireless router, you'll have to log in using a Web browser and look up the HEX key for your particular router.

The iPhone Doesn't Come On

Make sure that your battery is charged. Try either connecting it to your computer's USB port or to the AC adapter with the USB cable that came with the iPhone. The iPhone's screen should come on when it's connected to a power source and indicate that the battery is charging. If not, then you may want to try a soft reset. Press-and-hold the Home button and the Sleep/Wake button located on the top of the iPhone until you see the Apple logo. You can let go then and you should be back in business.

iTip

If you have an iPhone 3G, make sure you use the USB cable that came with it, as older cables and chargers may not be compatible. Also, older FireWire-based chargers will not charge the iPhone 3G.

No Sound

There could be several reasons why your iPhone isn't making any sounds. The first thing to check is that you don't have it on Silent. Check the Ring/Silent switch on the left side of the iPhone. Make sure it's pushed towards the front of the iPhone. If you see an orange dot on the switch, that means that it's on Silent. The next thing to check is the volume. Press the Volume Up button on the left side of the iPhone below the Ring/Silent switch (the Volume Up and Volume Down buttons are shown circled above). If you're not hearing your media content, then check to make sure the volume is turned up there, as well. Lastly, verify that the iPhone doesn't have anything plugged into its headset jack, or if you are using headphones, that they are pressed all the way in. Most headphones will not go all the way down into the iPhone's recessed headset jack. If you have your iPhone docked in an iPod or iPhone speaker system, make sure that the speaker system has power and is on.

Getting Better Reception

The iPhone 3G uses the latest and greatest 3G wireless chipset. However, depending on where you're located, you may not be in a great 3G coverage area. This can affect your phone reception. While all the cellular networks are working at breakneck speeds to get their networks updated, you may have to take measures in the meantime to improve your reception. One measure you can take is to simply turn 3G off. I know that it may sound like a really bad thing. After all, who doesn't want faster data? However, if you're not actively surfing the Web or using the Email app, then having 3G on is not really helping you. So try turning 3G off to see if that improves your reception in troubled areas. To turn 3G off, tap the Settings button on the Home screen, then tap General, and then tap Network. Tap the ON/OFF button to toggle 3G off.

Poor Phone Reception

Wi-Fi and
Bluetooth
Antenna
Areas

Antenna
Area

Cellular
Antenna
Area

First-generation iPhone

iPhone 3G

The iPhone doesn't use an external antenna. However, it does have an internal antenna.
It's located near the bottom on the back, under the black plastic cover. If you're in an
area with weak cellular coverage, then you might want to make sure that your hand
is not covering that plastic cover on the bottom of the first-generation iPhone. On the
iPhone 3G, the cellular antenna is located in the same area (on the back of the iPhone
near the dock connector). The Wi-Fi and Bluetooth antenna, however, is located near
the back-top edge of the iPhone 3G (and is integrated into the metal ring around the
camera, the audio jack, and the metal screen bezel). When you're riding in your car using
a Bluetooth headset or in-car Bluetooth hands-free, you might want to take the iPhone
out of your pocket or purse to get better reception.

Apple Bluetooth Headset Won't Connect

©ISTOCKPHOTO/MICHAEL KEMTER

Depending on the sequence in which you turned on your iPhone and your iPhone Blue-tooth Headset, the iPhone may not connect to the headset automatically. You can force the connection to happen by doing one of two things: First, try to simply tap the button on the back of the iPhone Bluetooth Headset and you'll hear a beep. Sometimes this is all you need to do to re-establish the connection. However, if that didn't do it, press-and-hold the iPhone Bluetooth Headset button for a few seconds, until you hear four descending tones. Release the button. This means that headset has been powered off. Now wait at least 10 seconds and power the headset back on by holding down the same button on the headset for a few seconds, until you hear four ascending tones. The headset has now been powered on and should make the connection.

The iPhone May Cause Interference

If you have other wireless devices in your home/office such as cordless phones, speaker systems, video/audio recording equipment, etc., the iPhone's transceiver could cause audible interference (buzzing) on these devices. If this happens, you can usually cure it by going to Settings (from the Home screen) and turning on Airplane Mode. However, note that while your iPhone is in Airplane mode, you will not be able to make or receive calls or access the Internet.

Turn It Off and Back On

Some problems can be cured by simply turning the iPhone off and back on again. To turn the iPhone off and back on, hold down the Sleep/Wake button on the top of the iPhone. After a few seconds, you will get a message that says Slide to Power Off. Go ahead and tap on the red arrow button, then slide your finger across to the right to power off the iPhone. Once the iPhone powers off, you can power it back on by holding down the Sleep/Wake button. Once the iPhone comes back on, you can try to do whatever it was that wasn't working before.

It's Not Responding

In the rare situation that your iPhone is on but not responding to your touch, you can reboot it. To reboot the iPhone, press-and-hold the Home and Sleep/Wake buttons simultaneously until you see the Apple logo. Then you can let go of these two buttons. The iPhone should boot up normally and return to normal operation.

Can't Make Calls

In order to make calls, your iPhone has to be active and there has to be a cellular network in range. Your carrier's name should be displayed in the upper-left corner, along with your current signal strength. If you're roaming on another provider's network, you should see that network's name. If you don't see a network name or you see No Service, then you will not be able to make calls until you are back in the range of a wireless carrier. Also, if you have traveled outside of your country's home network, you may not be set up for international roaming on your plan. Check with your carrier to make sure that your account has international roaming on it. Also make sure you're not in Airplane mode. If there is a little icon of a plane in the upper-left corner of the screen, then you are in Airplane mode and will not be able to make calls until you turn Airplane mode off in the settings (from the Home screen).

Did Your App Crash?

Not all applications are created equally, and therefore you may have an app crash on occasion. The good thing is that the iPhone is based upon Mac OS X, which is really reliable. So even if an app crashes, it usually won't affect the rest of the iPhone and will simply return you to the Home screen. However, if the app just appears frozen and not responding, then you can manually force quit it by pressing-and-holding the Home button on the front of the iPhone. Hold it down for at least six seconds, and you should be returned to the Home screen.

Do a Backup and Restore

If your iPhone is misbehaving or just plain acting weird, it may be time to do a restore. You'll need to sync your iPhone before doing this so that your iPhone is backed up. Once the sync is complete, leave your iPhone connected to your computer and click the Restore button on the Summary tab in iTunes. This will reinstall the current iPhone firmware on your iPhone and then do a restore of your data from the backup back onto your iPhone. This process can easily take 20 minutes or more, so make sure you do it when you have time to be without your iPhone.

Missing Album Art

You can download album art for the vast majority of your iTunes Music Library directly in iTunes. You do this by going to the Advanced menu and choosing Get Album Artwork. If you notice a bunch of missing album art in iTunes or on your iPhone, you can correct this by doing the following: In iTunes, select the tracks that are missing album art. Control-click (PC: Right-click) on them and choose Clear Downloaded Artwork. Control-click on them again and choose Get Album Artwork. iTunes will then download the album art for any tracks that you are missing artwork for that iTunes has in its catalog. Finally, re-sync your iPhone.

You're on Wi-Fi, but the iPhone Uses EDGE

This could be caused by a couple of different scenarios. It's possible that you entered your WEP password with a typo. It could also be caused by routers that use MAC address filtering and the MAC address for your iPhone hasn't been entered into the router's filter list. If you experience this problem, first verify that your password has been entered correctly. The easiest way to do this is to go to the Home screen and tap Settings, then tap Wi-Fi. Tap the blue arrow button next to the name of your network. Next, tap Forget This Network. Then try accessing your Wi-Fi network again and re-entering the password. If the WEP password is not being accepted, try entering the HEX key. If your router uses MAC address filtering, then you'll need to log onto your router's admin page and enter the iPhone's Wi-Fi MAC address, which can be found under General on the Settings screen. On the General screen, tap About and scroll down the screen.

Renew Your DHCP Lease Manually

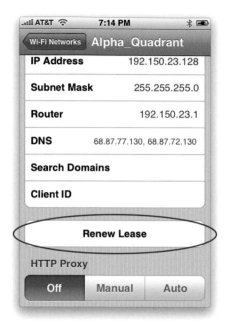

If you're connected to a commercial hot spot, like those at a favorite coffee shop or restaurant, and you're having problems getting out onto the Internet, try renewing your DHCP lease. Tap Settings from the Home screen and then tap Wi-Fi. Next, tap the blue arrow button for the network that you're connected to, scroll down, and tap the Renew Lease button. This will tell the iPhone to grab an updated IP address and possibly updated DNS info.

Battery Saving Tips

The iPhone has an impressive battery life. However, everyone's experience is going to be based upon how they use their iPhone. So there are ways to get a few extra hours out of the battery and to get close to the Apple specs for how long the battery should go between charges. Like anything else, any one of these tips will help, but the more of them you use, the longer your battery will go between charges.

- Try reducing the screen brightness. The iPhone's screen is one of the main sources for drawing power. If you reduce the brightness of the screen, the iPhone will use less battery power. You can do this from the Settings screen.
- Check mail less frequently or manually. Each time your iPhone checks for mail, it has to use the data network or Wi-Fi. Try setting the Auto-Check to a longer interval or turning it off, also from the Settings screen.
- Turn off Wi-Fi and Bluetooth, if not needed. If you're in an area that doesn't have Wi-Fi or are traveling on a train, then there is no reason to have the iPhone constantly searching for a network to connect to. Turn off Wi-Fi from the Settings screen. If you're not using a Bluetooth headset, you can turn off Bluetooth, too. With these radios off, the iPhone will also charge faster.
- As with most electronic devices that use rechargeable batteries, it's always a good idea to let your battery run completely down occasionally before recharging. Think of it as exorcising the battery and prolonging its life, as well.

More Battery Saving Tips

If you have an iPhone 3G, you have a couple more options to save battery life. The iPhone 3G can use your cellular provider's third-generation network for faster data speed. That's great, but if you're not actively surfing the Web, then having the 3G feature enabled is putting an unnecessary drain on your battery. Tap Settings from your Home screen, and then tap General. Next tap Network, and you'll see that Enable 3G is on by default. Tap the ON/OFF button to turn off 3G. This will improve your battery life. Also, whether you're on an iPhone 3G or the original iPhone with the iPhone 2.0 software or higher, you have the ability to have data "pushed" to your iPhone, such as email and calendar and contact updates. If you don't need this kind of real-time info, then you can switch from Push to Fetch. This will bring in your data on a timed interval, as opposed to every second of the day. I found that turning off Push gave me a drastic improvement on my iPhone 3G's battery life. You can turn Push off by tapping Settings from the Home screen and then tapping Fetch New Data. Lastly, if you don't need the location services (geotagging your photos, GPS, etc.), you can also extend your battery life by turning Location Services off in the General settings.

iPhone Not Seen by iTunes

In order to sync your iPhone to iTunes, you need to have iTunes version 7.7 or higher. If you're a Mac user, you also need to be on Mac OS X Tiger (version 10.4.10 or higher). There needs to be enough battery power for the iPhone to be able to turn on. If the iPhone's battery is completely drained, then you should charge it for at least 10 minutes before attempting to connect/sync it in iTunes. If that doesn't work, try plugging the iPhone into a different USB 2 port on your computer. If you're trying to use it with a USB hub, you may want to see if it works connected directly to your computer first. Try disconnecting other USB devices. If that doesn't work, try turning your iPhone off and back on before connecting to your computer.

SIM Card Not Detected by iPhone

SIM tray

The iPhone is a GSM-based phone and therefore comes with a SIM card already installed in it. If it's not being recognized by the iPhone, try removing it and re-seating it. Using a small paper clip or the SIM card removal tool that came with your iPhone 3G (you'll find it attached to the folder containing your Information Guide, etc.), insert one end in the hole on the SIM tray and press firmly until the SIM tray pops up. Make sure there is no dirt or debris on it and try putting it back in.

📶   **iTip**

If you ever have to send your iPhone in for service, you can remove the SIM card and try it in another GSM-based phone (this way, you'll still have use of a cell phone while yours is being serviced). Apple doesn't require your SIM card to service your phone and, as a matter of fact, they request that you remove it before you send it in anyway.

Software Updates Are Important

iPhone Software Update

Important Information

iPhone 2.1 Software Update

iPhone version 2.1 contains many bug fixes and improvements, including the following:
- decrease in call set-up failures and call drops
- significantly improved battery life for most users
- dramatically reduced time to backup to iTunes
- improved email reliability, notably fetching email from POP and Exchange accounts
- faster installation of 3rd party applications
- fixed bugs causing hangs and crashes if you have lots of 3rd party applications
- improved performance in text messaging
- faster loading and searching of contacts
- improved accuracy of the 3G signal strength display

Cancel   Previous   Next

While it's great that we can now sync our email, contacts, and calendars wirelessly via MobileMe and/or Microsoft Exchange, it's still a good idea to plug your iPhone into your Mac's or PC's USB port and do a sync every now and then. Not only will this back up your iPhone's data and settings, but it will also alert you to any software updates available from Apple. These software updates often contain important bug fixes and security updates to constantly improve your iPhone's performance.

Mac iCal & Address Book Sync Issues

With Mac OS X, the iPhone syncs directly to your contacts in Address Book and your calendars in iCal. If your syncing seems "stuck" and you've waited a decent amount of time with no movement, you may need to reset your sync history in iSync. Before you proceed I *highly recommend* that you back up both your Address Book and iCal files. To back up Address Book, open Address Book, go under the File menu, under Export, and choose Address Book Archive. This will make a complete backup file that you can use to revert back to of all your contacts. Open iCal and choose Back Up iCal from the File menu to back up your calendars. Once you have both Address Book and iCal backed up (you can also use a Time Machine backup for both), then launch iSync from your Applications folder. Choose Preferences from the iSync menu and then click the Reset Sync History button. This will reset your sync services data on your Mac. Then you can try syncing your iPhone again and it should sync the contacts and calendars successfully.

Get a Fresh Start with Your Information

If you want to wipe the Contacts, Calendars, Bookmarks, or Mail Accounts settings from your iPhone and replace them with what's currently on your computer, you can do this in iTunes. After you connect your iPhone to your computer, you can choose the Info preferences tab once your iPhone is selected in the Devices list. In the Advanced section, there is a checkbox for each of the above items that you can turn on to have iTunes overwrite what's currently on the iPhone with the contacts, calendars, bookmarks, or email account settings that are currently on your computer. This will be a one-time thing and the iPhone will sync normally on each subsequent connection.

Syncing Your iPhone with Entourage (Mac)

On a Mac, the iPhone only syncs directly with Mac OS X's Address Book, iCal, and your online Yahoo! Address Book. However, you can continue to use Microsoft Entourage as your primary personal information manager (PIM). The trick is that you have to use the latest version of Entourage from Microsoft Office 2004 or Entourage from Office 2008, which have support for Mac OS X Sync Services. To set this up, launch Entourage, go under the Entourage menu, choose Preferences, then go to the Sync Services preferences. Enable syncing for Address Book and Calendar. You will then be prompted on what to do with the first sync. If you don't have anything in Address Book or iCal, you can simply have Entourage overwrite those two with your Entourage contacts and calendar. This will sync all your contacts from Entourage to Address Book and your Entourage calendar will appear in iCal as a new calendar called "Entourage." Please note that it may take several minutes to populate Address Book and iCal if you have lots of information in Entourage. Both the Address Book and iCal applications will continue to sync with Entourage in the background. So if you add entries in either application, they will be synced back to Entourage and vice versa. Now you can sync your iPhone with Address Book and iCal because they will contain your info from Entourage.

Wiping the iPhone Completely

If you want to start completely from scratch on your iPhone and reset it back to its factory defaults, you can do so from the Settings screen. Tap Settings on the iPhone's Home screen, and tap General on the Settings screen. You will see a Reset button. Tap Reset and you will have a choice of Reset All Settings, Erase All Content and Settings, Reset Network Settings, Reset Keyboard Dictionary, Reset Home Screen Layout, and Reset Location Warnings. The main two settings that you'll want to choose from are Reset All Settings and Erase All Content and Settings. The first choice (Reset All Settings) will reset all your settings and preferences but leave your data and media intact. So you will still have all your contacts, calendars, songs, etc. The second option (Erase All Content and Settings) is the one that will reset the iPhone back to its factory defaults and wipe out everything you put on it.

Chapter Eleven
Setting Me Off
The Ins and Outs of Your iPhone's Settings

 I was a bit concerned about using the song title "Setting Me Off" for this chapter, because I thought it might sound too aggressive for a chapter on something as non-confrontational as learning about which iPhone settings do what. But then when I learned (by doing a quick search in the iTunes Store) that the group that recorded the song was named Speed\Kill/Hate (from their album *Acts of Insanity*), I felt much better about it. Well, that was until I noticed that the iTunes Store people had added an Explicit label beside the song's name (they do this as a warning to parents, because frankly kids couldn't care less. In fact, I imagine that when a teen sees an Explicit label beside a song, to them it means "This is for you!"). Anyway, once I saw that label, I did what any responsible adult would do—I double-clicked on it to hear the free 30-second preview. It was a heavy metal song and I have to be honest with you—I must be getting really old, because I couldn't understand a single word he sang. He could have been reading a *Sopranos* script set to music, containing every four-letter word known to merchant marines, and there is no possible way I would have been able to discern even one. Luckily, my son has a special CD player (generally used only by DJs) that lets you slow the speed of the CD down, and it was only then that I was able to hear the lyrics for the opening verse of "Setting Me Off," which were "Don't go changin'…to try and please me. You never let me down before… oooh, oooh, oooh…oooh, oooooh," so I felt pretty good about it.

Airplane Mode

Although it may be safe to move about the cabin, most airlines forbid you to have your phone (or any other device that transmits) on during flight. However, since the iPhone is more than just a phone, you'll probably want to use its other functions while in the air. Apple has your back on this one. They've included an Airplane mode. While in this mode, the phone, Wi-Fi, and Bluetooth transceivers are turned off. To switch to Airplane mode, tap the Settings button from the Home screen, and then tap on the word OFF next to Airplane Mode at the top to turn Airplane mode on. You'll always know you're in Airplane mode because there will be a little airplane icon in the upper-left corner where your carrier's logo used to be. Once you land, you can turn Airplane mode back off by tapping on the Airplane Mode ON button in the Settings screen to toggle it off.

---

iTip

Although Airplane mode was designed for use on airplanes, it's also useful in other situations, such as being near a P.A. system mic, or during a recording session, or being near your stereo speakers, where there may be interference from your GSM-based iPhone. If you start to hear a loud buzzing sound coming from these other sources, it may be your iPhone causing it. Go into Airplane mode to stop it.

Wi-Fi

The iPhone does a great job of seeking out and showing you a list of available wireless networks. By default, Wi-Fi is on. From the Wi-Fi Networks screen (from the Home screen, tap on Settings, then tap on Wi-Fi), you can turn Wi-Fi off or on by tapping on the ON/OFF button. You can also see the available networks that the iPhone sees and may be connected to. If there is a little Lock icon next to the network name, then that network is secured with a password. The iPhone supports both WEP and WPA security. So if you know the password (or HEX key for WEP), you can key it in and log on. If there is a network that you're near that isn't broadcasting its name (it's cloaked), you can tap Other, key in the network name, and choose the type of security the network is using so that you may key in the appropriate password or HEX key. Lastly, there is an Ask to Join Networks button. It's important to know about this one. While you're out and about, there may be lots of Wi-Fi networks in the area. When you go to use the data features of the iPhone, if the iPhone sees an open Wi-Fi network it will ask you to join it rather than using your carrier's 3G or EDGE network. Some may find this constant asking annoying. You can disable this so that the iPhone won't prompt you constantly to join networks. However, then it will be up to you to proactively check to see if there is a network available.

iPhone Usage

The Usage screen gives you a one-page summary of your iPhone usage (from the Home screen, tap on Settings, then tap on General, and then tap on Usage). It lists the amount of hours and minutes of usage and standby since your last full charge. This is great for tracking battery life. It will also show you your call time and your cellular network data usage. If you want to start tracking these statistics from scratch, just flick down to the bottom of the screen and tap the Reset Statistics button to start them over again at zero. Your Call Time and Cellular Network Data statistics will be reset. However, your Lifetime call time and battery usage will not be reset.

Choosing and Managing Sounds

The Sounds screen (from the Home screen, tap on Settings, then tap on Sounds) allows you to choose to turn your Vibrate setting on or off. By default, Vibrate is on for both the Silent and Ring modes. So whether you use the external Ring/Silent switch to turn the ringer on or off, the phone will vibrate when you receive a call. You can change the settings for both Silent and Ring independently of each other. You can also change your Ring volume here by dragging the little knob (circle) on the slider with the speakers on both ends. It's here that you also choose a default ringtone. The iPhone's default ringtone is Marimba. However, you can pick from a list of 25 different ringtones, and any custom ringtones you've added, by tapping Ringtone. The ringtone you pick is how the iPhone will ring for all incoming calls, except those of contacts that you've assigned custom ringtones to. The iPhone makes sounds every time you receive a new voicemail message, text message, email, or calendar alarm. It also makes sounds when you send email, tap on the keyboard, or when the iPhone locks. You can turn these sounds on or off individually for each area. For example, while I'm traveling I want to leave my phone on at night for emergency calls from home, but I don't want to hear a sound from every email or text message that comes in. So I turn off the sounds for New Mail and New Text Message before I go to bed. This way the iPhone won't make a sound unless I receive a call.

Adjusting the Brightness

The iPhone screen is very bright and it automatically adjusts the brightness under certain conditions to conserve battery life. However, if you want to manually adjust the brightness, you can. Tap the Brightness button in the Settings screen and drag the slider to the left to make the display dimmer or to the right to make it brighter. You can also disable the Auto-Brightness if you like by tapping on the ON/OFF button.

Changing Your Wallpaper

When you first turn on the iPhone or wake it from sleep, it displays a beautiful picture of the earth. However, if you want to choose a different picture or a picture of your own, you can. Tap the Wallpaper button in the Settings screen. You'll have a choice between the Apple-supplied wallpaper photos in the Wallpaper screen or your own photos that you either took with the iPhone camera or synced from your computer. Navigate any of these screens and choose the photo you want to use as your wallpaper. You'll be able to scale it using two fingers and move it around into position to get it the way you want. Once you have it looking the way you want, tap the Set Wallpaper button.

General Settings

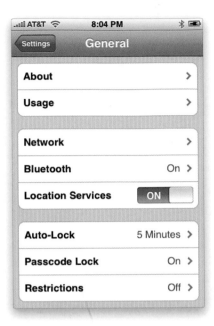

In the General settings screen within Settings, there is a lot of useful information. For example, tapping About gives you almost all the information you could use about your iPhone. You'll find things like the number of songs, videos, and photos that you have, as well as the amount of available space, serial number of the iPhone, software version, and firmware version. You'll also find all the MAC addresses for the Wi-Fi and Bluetooth chips. There are some other very useful items in the General settings, as well. You'll find a button to turn Bluetooth on and pair it with your headset or car kit, and in the Keyboard screen, you'll be able to turn on the Enable Caps Lock function (boy was I happy to find that one). You can even set up a four-digit password that would have to be typed in to unlock your iPhone. For those needing to set up a VPN (Virtual Private Network) connection to access their corporate network, you would do that on the Network screen. You'll need the VPN settings from your company's IT department. Lastly, if you have a teenager with an iPhone, you can set up some restrictions here by tapping Restrictions. You'll be able to restrict the iPod to not play content with explicit lyrics. You can prevent the use of Safari, YouTube, the iTunes Wi-Fi Store, and prevent the installation of apps. I know what you're thinking, "What's to stop them from turning these items back on?" When you tap the Enable Restrictions button, you'll first key in a four-digit passcode that only you will know. Set your restrictions and that four-digit passcode will be needed to get back in and make changes.

Don't Forget to Set Your Time Zone

If you travel to different time zones, you'll have to decide how you want the iPhone to handle the times for events in your calendar. For example, let's say you have an appointment set for 12:00 p.m. Eastern time. When you go to California, which is on Pacific time, do you want the event to display as 12:00 p.m. or 9:00 a.m.? If you leave Time Zone Support off, then the event will automatically adjust based upon the time zone you're in. So, your appointment would display as 9:00 a.m. If you want it to display the time you set the appointment for, no matter what time zone you're in, then you would turn Time Zone Support on and set your home/default time zone. Tap Settings from the Home screen and then tap Mail, Contacts, Calendars. Scroll down to the Calendar section and tap Time Zone Support. By default, Time Zone Support is on (if you wanted to turn it off, tap on ON). Tap Time Zone and key in your home/default city. If you live in a smaller town, it may not be in the list, so you may have to choose the largest city in your time zone instead.

Mail, Contacts, Calendars Settings

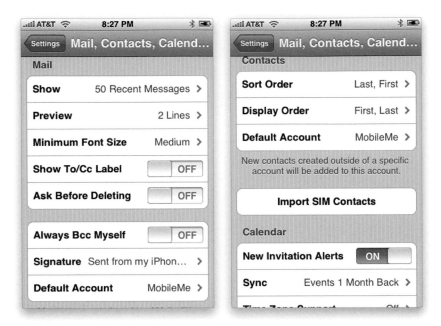

In the Mail, Contacts, Calendars settings screen within Settings, you can see, change, or add email accounts. However, you can also change the settings for the way the iPhone works with your existing email accounts, contacts, and calendars. By default, the iPhone shows you the 50 most recent messages. You can change this to 25, 75, 100, or 200. The iPhone shows you the first two lines of the incoming message without having to open the message. You can change it from zero to five lines. You can also choose your minimum font size here. This is important for those that have a hard time reading the smaller screen of the iPhone. You can turn on Show To/Cc Label of your incoming messages, which will put a little To or CC in front of your name to let you know if the message was sent to you or you were just carbon copied on it. When you delete a message on the iPhone, it does it immediately. However, if you'd like a warning, you can turn on the Ask Before Deleting button. If you want to have Mail always blind carbon copy you on your outgoing messages, you can turn on Always Bcc Myself. The iPhone puts a cool "Sent from my iPhone" message at the end of every message that you send out. You can edit this to say whatever you like by tapping the Signature button. You can also choose how your contacts are displayed and sorted and when you add new contacts, which account (if you have more than one) they will go into by default. If you're upgrading from a different kind of phone that stores the contacts on the SIM card, you can import those contacts. This is the screen that also lets you set options for your calendar alerts and how far back to sync events that have passed.

Phone Settings

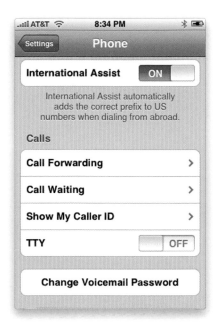

The first option in the Phone settings screen is pretty cool! Since the iPhone is a GSM-based phone, that means it works in other countries (make sure you call your carrier before you go abroad to have international roaming enabled on your account). I recently visited Italy and the first thing people wanted to do when we got off the plane was call home to let loved ones know that they made it. The hardest thing to figure out on their phones was what they needed to dial to call back to the States. The iPhone has a feature called International Assist that's on by default. This will automatically add the appropriate numbers to your calls back to the U.S. Under the Calls section, you can enable Call Forwarding to have your incoming calls automatically forwarded to another number. Call Waiting can be turned off so that if you're on a call and another call comes in, it will be sent to voicemail immediately. You can also turn off the Show My Caller ID feature. However, keep in mind that many people don't accept calls from numbers that are blocked. For the hearing impaired, you can turn on the TTY (Teletypewriter) feature. Apple does sell an iPhone TTY adapter separately that allows you to connect your iPhone to teletype machines. You can change your voicemail password here in the Phone settings screen, as well. The last two options are SIM PIN and the Services screen for your provider. Enabling a SIM PIN makes it harder for someone to take your SIM card and use it in another phone. If your provider uses the Services menu, you'll be able to access things like speed dial numbers to check your bill balance and directory assistance.

Safari Settings

Using the Safari settings screen, you can change your default search engine. If you prefer Yahoo search over Google search, you can change that here. By default, the iPhone has JavaScript, Plug-Ins, and Block Pop-Ups on. You can turn each of these off if you need to. The iPhone's Safari Web browser is also set to accept cookies from visited sites. Other than Never, this is probably the safest setting. Cookies are good in the fact that they minimize the need on many sites to have to constantly log in. Your login info or site settings can be stored as a cookie right in your iPhone's Safari browser. Lastly, in the Safari settings, you can choose to clear your browsing history, Clear Cookies, and Clear Cache to basically remove any trace of your having been to the sites you've been to.

iPod Settings

There are four iPod Music settings to choose from in the iPod settings screen: The first one is Sound Check. With Sound Check on, the iPhone's iPod application attempts to balance the sound levels of your songs. So, for example, if you have one song that is really loud and another song that isn't so loud, with Sound Check on it should lower the volume of the really loud song and raise the volume of the song that isn't so loud. The next setting is for your audiobook speed. If you prefer to speed up or slow down your audiobook playback, you can change the default from Normal to Faster or Slower. The third setting is for EQ (equalizer). It's possible (and recommended) to set the EQ setting for each of your songs in iTunes. You can set all your rock tracks to the Rock EQ setting, all your R&B to the R&B EQ setting, all your jazz to the Jazz EQ setting, etc. When they are played on the iPhone, they'll sound better. You can also set a default EQ setting for the songs that don't have an EQ setting. You can only pick one, so pick the one that would cover the bulk of your music collection. In the last Music setting, you can set a volume limit. This can help those who are concerned that they may suffer hearing loss if the music is too loud. This will limit the volume across the board, and there's even a four-digit security code that you can assign to it so your teenager can't go back in and just turn it off. By default, your videos will start playing from where you left off. However, if you'd like them to play from the beginning, you can change that here in the iPod Video settings. If the video you're playing has closed captioning, you can choose to display it here, as well.

Setting Your Options for the Photos Application

There are four basic settings for the Photos application. The first setting allows you to set the duration for each photo during your slide shows. The default is 3 seconds, but you can set it from 2 to 20 seconds. The next setting lets you choose your default slide transition. You can choose between Cube, Dissolve (the default), Ripple, Wipe Across, and Wipe Down. The third option is Repeat. By default, this is off, which means that your slide show will stop after the last slide. You can turn on Repeat so that it loops the slide show. The last option is Shuffle, which is off by default. With Shuffle on, your slide shows will play in a random order.

Settings for Your Third-Party Applications

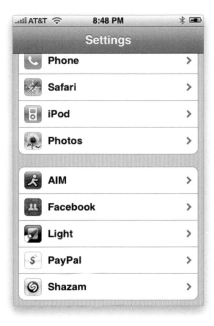

If you have any third-party applications on your iPhone, the developer may have included settings that you can configure. These apps will be at the bottom of the main Settings screen. Just tap the app that you wish to adjust. If you delete the app, the settings for that app will also be deleted.

Index

T

U

V